INTO A WIDER WORLD

FRIENDS, FAMILY, AND ALLIES
COMPANIONS FOR THE JOURNEY

Other books by Karl E. Lutze:

To Mend the Broken

Forgive Our Forgettings, Lord!

Of Walls and Doors

A Lot on My Mind, Lord

Awakening to Equality

We Need to Talk, Lord!

INTO A WIDER WORLD

FRIENDS, FAMILY, AND ALLIES
COMPANIONS FOR THE JOURNEY

KARL E. LUTZE

MAVEN
MARK
BOOKS

Milwaukee, Wisconsin

Published by
MavenMark Books
An imprint of HenschelHAUS Publishing, Inc.
www.henschelHAUSbooks.com

ISBN: 978159598-349-7
E-ISBN: 978159598-350-3
LCCN: 2014954296

Publisher's Cataloging-In-Publication Data
(Prepared by The Donohue Group, Inc.)

Lutze, Karl E.
Into a wider world : friends, family, and allies-- companions for the journey /
Karl E. Lutze.
pages : illustrations ; cm
Includes index.
Issued also as an ebook.
ISBN: 978-1-59598-349-7
1. Lutze, Karl E.--Friends and associates. 2. Lutheran Church--Oklahoma--
Clergy--Biography. 3. African American churches--Oklahoma--History--20th
century. 4. Civil rights movements--Oklahoma--History--20th century. 5.
College teachers--Indiana--Biography. 6. Autobiography. I. Title.
E185.98.L88 A3 2014 284.1092   2014954296

Cover photography by Professor Peter C. Lutze
Cover design by Assistant Professor Yeohyum Ahn

Printed in the United States of America.

TRIBUTE

Eileen and I are honored to be able to sponsor the publication of Karl Lutze's newest book, ***Into A Wider World–Friends, Family, and Allies –Companions for the Journey***. The message of this book should be available for generations to come, not just for Karl's great-grandchildren, but for all of our posterity.

The publication of this book we dedicate to you, Karl Lutze. Karl, you have been a friend for many years, but more than that, you are my hero, my champion, my model. I am inspired by your constant attention to the matters at hand—the recognition that our real first commandment is to take care of our brothers and sisters.

You have championed the call to care for those who cannot speak for themselves. You have rung the bell so many times in so many places. Your welcome to the alien and the outsider constantly reminds me to remember my calling to welcome the stranger.

Thank you, Karl, for your friendship, and for using your God-given gifts so well.

John Frerking

THANK YOU TO ALL WHO HELPED

Natalie Thiele

Carol Lobes

Kathleen Mullen

Betsy Eggers Honderd

John Frerking

Bob and Shirley Zimmer

John and Marilyn Kleinhans

Fred Niedner

Yeohuyn Ahn

Peter, Steve, Tom, and
Mark Lutze

Dorothy Warner

And, of course, Gail ...

KARL E. LUTZE

TABLE OF CONTENTS

INTRODUCTION

In days past, when pulling together material to be included in other books I've written, I've found it useful to ask helpful people to glance at and comment on prepublication manuscripts and to make suggestions. For "openers," each of those friendly folk would invariably ask me, "What audience of readers do you envision?"

For *this* book, I raised the question myself. I couldn't come up with an easy answer.

In my musings, the realization struck me that I really had little knowledge about either of my grandfathers, both of whom had died long before my birth. And about their parents and households I know almost nothing.

I have grandchildren of my own now, so it is not unlikely that someday some of these may have grandchildren too. It is highly unlikely that such yet-to-be-born offspring will know much about their kinfolk of my generation, and they might welcome a chat with me to learn about us and some happenings in my life and in the lives of people who touched mine.

In addition, there are glimpses into the history of the Lutheran Church, Valparaiso University, and the civil rights quest. As you read you will also find vignettes of persons of special courage.

You'll probably not find what I've written here in public libraries or book stores. So if you'd be willing to save some space on one of your bookshelves for a copy of these pages, you might be helping me to make possible some intergenerational conversation. I'd be pleased

* * * * *

The word *bombarded* came to mind when I began to reflect on my days after leaving Oklahoma and arriving in Valparaiso in September, 1959. However, that term suggested to me violence, devastation, and destruction.

Then the analogy of a giant maple tree seemed more appropriate—thousands of little propeller-like seedlings whirling around gently to the ground, countless of them actually grounded into the earth and sprouting into tiny stems bearing leaves. No, that notion was less adequate in depicting what was really happening to me.

What I was to experience was more like a barrage of tennis balls being fired at me from all sides by mechanical pitching machines—not really a painful ordeal, but more, a series of persistent situations and circumstances that allowed for little rest or complacency—these nudged and pushed and pulled and stretched me.

It was like grasping for a handle on a whirling merry -go-round—exciting, terrifying, exhilarating, delightful, exhausting, as one holds on for dear life, not knowing when it would stop or where. But you cannot get off.

And you don't really want to get off.

PART I:

BREAKING NEW GROUND

CHAPTER 1

ANDREW SCHULZE

In 1945, I was only three months into my role as an ordained pastor "serving a Negro community in Muskogee, OK" (as my letter of assignment stated) when I got to meet the Reverend Andrew Schulze of St. Louis. He was pastor of Saint Philip, the largest Lutheran Congregation serving African-Americans at that time. He wasted little time on small talk, but welcomed me into what he believed must be seen as a clearly focused ministry marked by the Scripture. He had discovered in all his years of ministry that the greatest obstacle he faced in serving among people of color was the obvious advantage and deference accorded to White people and the subsequent inherent subordination of non-Whites.

He showed a special interest in the similarity between the ministry that he had developed in St. Louis and the ministry which we had just begun in Oklahoma. And he was eager to expand on describing his commitment to changes in the way such ministry was undertaken. He saw a need to note the current structures of

"White missionary work" in Black communities as being quite different from the Scriptural model that calls for a genuine loving of the neighbor and a welcoming of the "stranger within your gates." He pointed to the pattern for regarding the "outsider" discernible in the conduct and style of Jesus in his own ministry marked by such words as "come unto Me", and in gesturing towards people in the crowds that came to hear him. He said "Look—these are my brothers and sisters and my mother and my parents." He treated them as members of his family.

In lectures and in writings, he had kept pressing church leaders to attend to what he was exposing as a major flaw in the attitudes, structures, practices, and message of the churches and in the lives of their members as well.

Together with several fellow Lutherans—lay and clergy—Black and White—he had organized the St. Louis Lutheran Society for Better Race Relations. In addition to preparing, and distributing in Lutheran circles, tracts addressing race relations issues, the group sponsored an Institute on Race Relations in one of the larger St. Louis churches.

It was clear that most Whites, though they might not have been outright die-hard segregationists, nonetheless were comfortable with the "separate-but-equal" concept (in most cases emphasizing the *separate,* while soft-pedaling the *equal*). And most pastors and church leaders found themselves uncomfortable and often threatened by Schulze's persistent call for self-scrutiny and change.

This was the time of massive demographic changes. The United States' intense and expanded involvement in World War II resulted in unprecedented heavy demands by the military for vehicles, arms, and other materials. The large industrial centers of the North especially found manufacturers extending themselves, many of their factories open night and day, operating on three eight hour shifts each day of the week, including Sundays.

Now Black workers—and women, too—who had had far fewer employment opportunities in the past—and especially in the South—were suddenly being lured to fill the posts. Chicago was especially affected by the dramatic influx of African American workers and their families.

Church officials of the Northern Illinois District of the Lutheran Church-Missouri Synod (LCMS) became well aware of this phenomenal change. However, it was clear that the longtime all-White congregations weren't about to invite their new neighbors from the South to come to their churches.

Having learned of and hearing about Andrew Schulze's success in building a strong congregation in St. Louis, these officials decided to call on him to accept the responsibility of developing an appropriate ministry to meet the challenge presented by Chicago's burgeoning South Side, where most of these immigrants from the South had found living quarters.

Schulze, a far-sighted, hard-working, dedicated pastor, did establish one new small congregation in a crowded neighborhood where almost all of the residents were African-Americans. He became pastor of Christ the

King Lutheran Church. But also—just as he had done while in St. Louis—he organized the Chicago *Lutheran Society for Better Race Relations*. And he wanted to offer an Institute on Human Relations again, just as he had in St. Louis.

Northern Illinois District Officials had intended him to plant churches in "Negro Neighborhoods," and had not bargained for this man's endeavors to get existing churches to open their doors to *My Neighbor of Another Color* (title of the book Schulze had written while still in St Louis). These church officials, as well as the members and pastors of nearby congregations, found this man and his mission most unwelcome and threatening. They simply did not appreciate his confronting people in their unwillingness to accept the challenge of eliminating the practice of exclusiveness in the matter of race.

President O. P. Kretzmann of Valparaiso University, an independent Lutheran school, 50 miles from Chicago, had years earlier been one of Schulze's teachers when Andrew was still a seminary student at Springfield, IL. Kretzmann appreciated this courageous pastor's efforts, and recognized the resistance he had been encountering.

Expressing his own desire to make a public statement on behalf of the University to affirm such efforts as being faithfully Christian, President Kretzmann invited Schulze to proceed with plans for a weekend Institute. He was to schedule it for the following summer on Valparaiso's campus, inviting people from all over the country to participate.

The gathering proved an immediate success and plans were begun to establish this as an annual event to be called the Valparaiso University Institute on Human Relations. Furthermore, participants decided to establish a new organization, national in scope, to be called the *Lutheran Human Relations Association of America* (LHRAA). Institute participants chose Dr. Schulze to be the new organization's Executive Director. A Board of Directors was chosen and Valparaiso's President Kretzmann invited the Board to hold its meetings on the University's campus.

As I recall, about two years later, in a phone call, Pastor Schulze asked me to permit him to place my name as nominee to serve as a member of LHRAA's Board of Directors. I explained my surprise, reminding him that though I was a member of the Association and wanted to be supportive of its ministry, I had never even attended any of its annual Institutes.

He responded that he had stayed informed about my particular ministry in Oklahoma and its development; furthermore, he was eager to have on his Board people from different parts of the country and who also had first hand experiences in race relations concerns. Only a short time later, I was informed that I had been elected to LHRAA's Board.

At one of the first Board meetings I attended, Dr. Kretzmann sat at the table with us. After listening to some of the reports, most of them exposing the struggles the young organization was experiencing, he raised his hand and said, "It seems to me that most of your start-up problems could be dealt with, were you to have a salaried executive who could devote more time to the organizing and administering of the Association's program."

All of us nodded heads in agreement, but several of the group raised the problem of supporting a salaried executive because of the meager assets of the young organization.

Kretzmann responded that he had already considered that concern and was prepared to make an offer to deal with that obstacle: if the Association would accept the responsibility to pay half the salary of the executive, Valparaiso University was prepared to provide office space, and to help with salary by engaging that person as a half-time member of its Theology Department, acknowledging the University's right to participate in selecting the person to occupy that position.

While the rest of the members of the Board expressed delight at his words, I alone voiced misgivings, and indicated that the person named to that assignment by the University might not prove to be the choice of our Board—who would obviously be Dr. Schulze. Dr. Kretzmann in soft voice responded, "We have Dr. Schulze in mind."

And, blushing, I quickly joined the others in unanimous and grateful acceptance of the generous offer.

As I reflected on this new situation for LHRAA, I remembered my first introduction to Otto Paul Kretzmann and Valparaiso University.

CHAPTER 2
VALPARAISO UNIVERSITY —
LHRAA AND PRESIDENT O.P. KRETZMANN

After my seminary graduation and ordination in 1945, I began my ministry in an African-American community in Muskogee, OK. The only member of Hope Lutheran Church who was over twenty but under fifty was Dorthy Hooper, a graduate of Manual Training High School. She played piano for our worship services.

She lived in a four room house crowded together with her aging parents, a seventh grader niece, a teenage nephew, and their unemployed mother. Wages from Dorthy's employment, working the hot press of a downtown dry cleaning establishment, added to the pitifully small welfare check her aging father received each month. Income from her work helped make the family's survival possible.

I have no idea where she had cultivated her keyboard skills but I was impressed with her ability to sight-read music. She spent many hours at the church since the Hoopers had no piano in their home. In our frequent conversations she taught me much about the community and its culture.

Dorthy seemed to have many of the talents that would warrant her pursuing a college education. I was hardly qualified to be a career counselor, but I asked whether she had ever given thought to applying for admission to any college. The idea excited her.

We talked more about it in the weeks that followed. I agreed to explore possibilities—though I hardly had any idea where or how to begin. There must be dozens of ways to check out various options. Certainly the most promising procedure would NOT be to first contact the president of a college or university.

But I did.

OTTO PAUL KRETZMANN Although I had never met him, but had only heard about him, I sent off a letter to Dr. Otto Paul Kretzmann, President of Valparaiso University, about which, at that time, I knew hardly anything at all. To my surprise, he graciously—and personally—responded to my letter of inquiry that same week.

He explained that the University was eager to enroll talented young people of strong Christian character and a readiness to learn. He had gathered from my letter that Dorthy Hooper was just such a person. And then in his letter he begged for time.

He explained that no Negroes lived in Valparaiso, and, accordingly, no Negro students had yet been enrolled at the University. Apologizing, he explained that residents of the town harbored a strong hostility towards the very idea of people of color coming to their city.

Then he expressed his personal commitment to effecting a change in such attitudes. And he divulged his strategy: in a nation-wide involvement in and patriotic support of the country's military efforts and in the spirit of the time, he had arranged for the University to offer refresher courses for men who had been serving in the military chaplaincy.

The townsfolk, he reasoned, would be proud of a local educational institution offering such a service and, of course, incidentally, some of these chaplains would be African-Americans. Thus, his plan would serve as a wedge in the structure of racial exclusiveness that marked the city's social patterns. After that, he hoped, the campus would have turned the corner in enrolling students of color.

I hurried to share the news with Dorthy, only to learn she had just accepted the proposal of Homer Hamilton, a fine, handsome, young veteran who had captured her heart. So a college education was no longer a priority item in Dorthy's life plan. And my first contact with Valparaiso ended somewhat abruptly. The Hamiltons' wedding, by the way, was the very first wedding I performed.

I had not ever been to Valparaiso nor had I known any of its history. In about 1957, upon my first visit to the campus, I learned about Valparaiso's earlier days. The school's founders had taken on the challenge of starting a college that offered opportunity to study in a variety of fields—medicine, teacher training, business, law, even embalming. When a student's money allotted for meals, lodging, and tuition was exhausted, the student would receive a statement of certification that specified what courses had been completed.

College education became accessible and students enrolled by the hundreds. As the school provided only one residence hall, this was the moment for local residents to benefit from the enterprise. Reminders of those days are still standing near the original site of the campus. People built additions to their houses –- not always architectural jewels, but, for a significant number, an economic boon, because they were now renting rooms to students.

World War One's call for high school graduates to serve in the country's military efforts seriously diminished the number of enrollees applying for admission to the Valparaiso institution. Furthermore, prospective college-bound students more and more wanted their education from an accredited institution. VU had not yet developed an accreditation process. With increasing awareness of the impending collapse of the school, its best faculty members accepted positions in more prosperous schools. The count of students fell drastically. In the 1920s the word was out. The student body had shrunk in size to fewer than 1000; the school was up for sale, and only two parties had shown an interest in offering bids.

The first interest was shown by the Ku Klux Klan, notorious for its anti-Negro stance and record of violence (including cross-burning, and lynching) and its influence was spreading. A rumor was out that the Klan was buying VU. Hopes of neighborhood homeowners were revived. Their rooms would once again be filled. They were ready to sing "Happy Days Are Here Again!" The Klan was their rescuing hero, their friend who saved the day.

But the celebration had a short life.

Another announcement followed. The head of the Klan (who lived in Indiana) had been convicted of a serious criminal act. It was a shameful hour for the Klan, and the organization was without funds to purchase the school.

The second group emerged: Midwestern Lutherans, lay and clergy, with exceedingly limited finances. They were troubled that their Lutheran Church–Missouri Synod was willing to provide education for post-high schoolers only to prepare them to become clergymen and/ or teachers in parochial schools. The group called itself the Lutheran University Association and they purchased the school in 1925.

The Lutherans took bold steps to select from their midst the school's first two presidents, for short consecutive terms. Doctors Dau (1926-1929) and Kreinheder (1930-1939) set the course of the school in a sound direction. First, on March 13, 1929, the University was declared an accredited university. Their next important contributions to the future lay in their desire to engage a faculty who had themselves pursued their doctoral degrees. In 1940, they found a man with experience in higher education and who had also successfully headed up LCMS's nationwide program for cultivating the church's youth—O.P. Kretzmann. The institution that had almost wilted was once again revived.

Under his leadership the Walther League, a program developed for young adults in the LCMS, became a highly respected program of the church and the school became a university recognized by its peers in the secular education world.

Early on, VU's new President took note of the need to address the local demographic realities that both the city of Valparaiso and the University faced. In conversation, Pastor Ed Wessling, who in 1959 had been installed to serve as minister of Valparaiso's Immanuel Lutheran Church, shared with me his experiences upon arriving in Valparaiso. He told of his initial effort to meet all the Immanuel members and to learn what their personal needs might be. He mounted the stairs of one house and met the woman who lived there. He described her as "sweet, fragile, and grandmotherly." She welcomed her new pastor warmly and said, "Oh, Pastor, you will like it here in Valparaiso. There are no colored people living here!"

It didn't take a professional survey for even the most casual visitor to the city to discover that people of color were not welcome here, that Valparaiso, Indiana, was off limits to them. However, instead of delegating the task of tackling the problems of racial exclusiveness to some member of his staff or to some committee, the new University President chose to be personally involved in becoming an agent of change.

It was the end of summer in 1947. O.P. Kretzmann left the campus—his car—and made his way afoot to the Pennsy train station to await the arrival of the train from Philadelphia. As the train screeched to a halt he walked to the open door of the coach to assist Miss Inez Parker with the huge, heavy bag she was trying to lower.

Who was this celebrity? This was the young woman who in 1951 would be the first African-American student to graduate from Valparaiso University!

Carrying her heavy bag, O.P. Kretzmann escorted Inez Parker to the campus. Instead of going directly on a diagonal, short-cut route to the campus, they together went a block north to Lincolnway Avenue. They walked the city's main street as their route to the school. Peeking from behind curtains and in some instances stepping outside their little shops all could see this president of VU carrying her suitcase, personally welcoming her. This highly respected leader in the community had made his statement and the message was clear. When the occasion called for standing up to be counted, OP was there.

This was the man and this was the university that gave a home to LHRAA and to the Lutze family.

Years later, after I had become a part of the university faculty and was working with LHRAA and its Director, Dr. Andrew Schulze, and simultaneously teaching

Theology, there was another instance which revealed OP's personal commitment to be involved in efforts to respond to the turmoil and tensions in race relations.

By the 1970s, almost all major cities in the country were experiencing the pain of disruption and hostility. Misunderstanding and fear, distrust and suspicion marked attitudes that fanned the flames of division.

Sixty miles away in Chicago, young men and boys were declaring their identity, claiming certain sections of the city as their own turf, assuming leadership roles and asserting their position of power. They were defying authorities that they deemed unfair. They were ultimately regarding law enforcement presence as the enemy.

More often than not, these organized groups were referred to as gangs—a decidedly negative term suggesting lawlessness and criminality. The truth, however, was quite the opposite. One such organized movement, which chose as its name The Blackstone Rangers, initiated a breakfast program in collaboration with Southside churches to feed impoverished youngsters so that they might have a nourishing meal rather than having to make their way to school hungry, unprepared for the day's studying and learning.

A phone call from George Hrbek, LHRAA's staff member in Chicago, relayed a message he had received from a member of the Blackstone Rangers. The caller had explained that an annual holiday and picnic day for African-Americans on Chicago's South Side had been held each August since 1923. This special event, Bud Billiken

Day, was scheduled for the very next week. The caller explained it was likely that police would be present in large number and "they'd likely be doing some knocking of heads." George asked, "Would it be possible for us to bring a few busloads of kids to the campus of Valpo for a picnic day in a safe setting? We'd bring the food!"

At VU summer classes had ended. Students had left. Now almost fifty years since the inception of Bud Billiken Day, the Blackstone Rangers were proposing a joint venture to make the all day picnic a reality for a few busloads of kids ages 6 to 14. When I told Dr. Kretzmann about it, he registered immediate and enthusiastic support of the idea. The next thing we knew, we had marked off baseball diamonds, set up volleyball nets, and made arrangements for VU student swimmers to be on hand for supervising the swimming pool. Dr. Kretzmann had also authorized the Physical Education Department to provide equipment: gloves, balls, bats, and such.

When the buses finally arrived that Saturday morning, dozens of teenagers and younger children spilled onto the campus. They were wild with their new, spacious freedom, but the stern-voiced, no-nonsense leaders shepherded them in firm discipline to places where they were given their briefing and assignments for play.

At mealtime, they gathered at the bleachers in the football field. The guest leaders spread out their sumptuous fare. University food services had prepared gallons of lemonade. Next to the dispenser OP stood, greeting the young visitors, one at a time, while his dear wife, Flora was filling and refilling their paper beverage cups. And when lunch was over, the leaders picked up all the scraps of paper napkins, cups, and wrappers. They mounted their buses. It was an unforgettable day.

It was reassuring in the roles Andrew and I filled with LHRAA and the University to have a leader of the institution so very supportive of us in our committed purpose to weed out segregation, racism, and discrimination patterns so widespread in our country.

The Institutes that LHRAA held at Valparaiso University had begun before the LHRAA office was actually on campus. In the summer of 1959 (as the tenth of Andrew's annual Institutes was held, with 225 in attendance), the partnership with the University had already proven to be very successful.

The way in which Andrew structured the Institutes (including those he had conducted before bringing the event to VU's campus) revealed his leadership abilities. Each year, the agenda made room for assessing what was going on in race relations everywhere—in government, in commerce, in the churches, in the education world, in the North and in the South, calling on speakers who were personally involved in addressing the issues of interracial confrontations as well as people who were studying the various related aspects of concern.

What particularly pleased and energized Andrew was that people attending these meetings came from so many different—often distant—places, with different perspectives, and took time to participate in these sessions. He purposely would single out certain participants who he thought would be effective in pressing for church folk at the local level to become actively involved in enlisting others in chapters of LHRAA. He recruited twelve such persons he felt might be capable of enlisting interest groups in their local communities upon their return home.

Our annual Summer Institutes at the University were more than academic programs on race relations topics. They were designed to meet the needs of church officials and administrators who themselves had neither experience nor formal preparation that equipped them to deal with difficult, challenging human relations issues, such as those issues which impinged upon these leaders' particular fields of service.

The Institutes also attracted non-professionals from different areas, who were struggling with problems of racial tensions in the course of their everyday living. Here they could share their stories and encourage and affirm one another for renewed commitment to service. There really was no other such program designed and offered in the greater Lutheran community. So the number attending each year increased, and demanded a greater investment of staff time in planning and promoting.

Since Andrew himself had already founded twelve chapters of the Association in major cities across the country, each with only a handful of members, the workload—coupled with the opportunities for expansion that lay ahead—were more than could be reasonably expected of LHRAA's leader. It became apparent then that Dr. Schulze needed help.

That prompted LHRAA's Board, in 1959, to create a position of "Field Secretary" to share in the responsibilities of the Executive Director. University President Kretzmann concurred in the plan and agreed to enact the same arrangement that had been structured for Dr. Schulze: this new staff member would also teach half-time in the University's Department of Theology and half of his salary would be provided in that way. That is the position I was invited to fill.

The very thought of my returning to the classroom—this time as teacher—was both sobering and a bit intimidating.

It's not as if I had had no opportunity to learn and to grow intellectually, once I had completed my seminary courses. Personal study, reading periodicals, doing research for lectures and more formal presentations at conferences and other speaking engagements, and of course sermon preparation, had made studying a vital factor in pursuing my position as pastor. A pastor I was, and the best possible pastor I wanted to be, intending to serve my congregation and the larger community wherever that might be. I really therefore had no pressing urge to pursue a formal, disciplined academic regimen that would ultimately mark me as degreed—a certified scholar.

In joining the staff of LHRAA I really didn't relieve Andrew. He still worked long hours and late nights. He simply kept doing what he loved doing and did well. My task was to chip away on the long list of things he had always hoped to tackle but lacked time to carry out. Of course that called for my traveling to over thirty more cities where we organized additional chapters. And that meant driving and flying to those sites. And that meant enlisting more volunteers at local levels, visiting prospective supporters, submitting proposals to foundations to make possible programs of service, publishing materials for use in congregations, writing articles for the *VANGUARD*, LHRAA's bi-monthly newsletter, and other periodicals.

When I'd go to a distant city, I'd try to squeeze in as many meetings as I could to make each dollar spent achieve maximum returns. On one particular occasion, I had an evening meeting with members of the St. Louis Chapter of LHRAA. I had been scheduled to meet with Missouri Synod President Oliver Harms early next morning and with members of his staff throughout the afternoon. When these would end, Dr. Roland Sebold was to drive me to Lambert Field, where we'd agreed to have an airport dinner before my take off and return to Chicago. We'd known each other well in our days as seminary students and there had been a good many changes in our lives through the years.

Most recent—and exciting—for him was being named editor of Concordia Publishing House, the official printing establishment of LCMS. After hearing him describe the details of his new post, I chided him a bit and asked him, "Rol, do you know that in the dozens of years of publishing, Concordia has never put out a book on race relations?"

His quick answer: "No one has ever submitted a manuscript." And then he added, "Why don't you?"

I responded, "Since I would be favoring desegregation, and since there's been reluctance by the church officials to get into areas that might produce conflict, anything I would write would be returned to me for alterations, omissions and suggested revisions. I wouldn't have time for that."

His simple reply, "Try us!"

The public address system announced the boarding time for my departure and I had a lot to think about for the ride home.

I must have started writing that book a dozen times. Maybe more.

Time started to slip by. There were other "must do" items tugging at me. The next trip was going to be my doorway to getting things done.

It was early in 1965 and I was scheduled for a trip that included Los Angeles and San Diego. As usual, I had certain tasks to attend to while there and a stopover on my return was scheduled for Denver, when I was to meet with Board members of the Wheat Ridge Foundation before heading back to Chicago—and, at last, home.

I took a brief rest from the pre-boarding rush to enjoy a smooth take-off and what promised to be a good trip. Once we were airborne, I removed my writing pad from my briefcase, laid it on my tray table and, pen in hand,

and I started writing. No phone calls, no interruptions—a smooth ride. I had a window seat. And when I raised my head to enjoy the view, what I saw was a flashing of flames spewing from one of the plane's great engines.

I called out to the flight attendant who was walking the aisle nearby, "That engine out there—is that the way it's supposed to be?* She rushed to the pilot's cabin.

Things became somewhat hushed among the passengers. Their uneasiness was quickly discernible.

After communicating with his crew, and with his flight coordinators on the ground, the pilot then announced that the flight tower had ordered our return to Los Angeles. We would board another flight that was being readied for a flight to Denver. With that, he steered our ship into an about-face swoop and we were on our way back to LA. Although annoyed that plans of all on board had to be altered, we were relieved that we seemed to be out of a dangerous situation.

We were getting close to the landing strip in LA when our pilot rather apologetically informed us that the very plane we were to take had just left. These were pre-cell-phone days so, once we'd landed, people were crowding the phone booths to adjust their personal schedules.

When I telephoned the Wheat Ridge people, they told me that once they heard of my flight troubles, they had canceled the meeting. I had already been booked to Denver, so I continued on the next available flight.

Once in Denver, I went to the motel I had reserved prior to my leaving Valpo. The meeting had been canceled; my return flight ticket was flexible enough to offer me several options for deciding what to do or where to go.

The evening was mine, no agenda, no responsibilities, even though I was hardly relaxed after all the hustling and shake-up of my day. I had friends in Denver—Konemans, Lowes, Neeses, Brueggemanns, Pollacks, Lasses, and other former VU students, yet as I opened my travel bag, my pen and writing pad dropped to the floor—a strong suggestion that I stay right there and do some writing.

It pained me to be in Denver and not be able to contact friends there, but I resisted the urge and even extended my stay in the motel three extra days until I completed the manuscript. They were very long days, from early morning to late nights. Once I had returned to my office and my staff had typed what I had written, it was ready to go off to my friend at Concordia. He called me back only a few days later to thank me for the work I'd done and to tell me he anticipated no hurdles the new book, *To Mend the Broken,* would encounter on its way to the press. The book was published by Concordia in 1966.

Writing the book was not what I expected my work with LHRAA to be, but it gave me time to think about the larger implications of our work. As I had stated in the book it was necessary for all of us to see that we, White Christians, were as much a part of the problems as the solution-finders.

In the first years at Valparaiso, Dr. Schulze had laid a foundation of serving the University and doing follow up on human relations work. So when congregations not too distant from Valparaiso wanted a guest preacher for a particular Sunday, Andrew and I would respond as helpfully as possible.

In my first months in Indiana, I don't recall any formal, detailed statement coming my way explicitly outlining what was expected of me in my new position. A note now and then on my desk from Andrew would apprise me of some task I should perform. Or a phone call from Bob Bertram, chair of VU's Theology Department, would notify me of some procedure I should attend to for the Theology Department. It wasn't as if there was nothing to do. If anything, the piles of items mounting on my desk called for arriving early each day and spending long hours in the evening.

On one of those evenings, I received a phone call from Bob Clausen. I'd known him in seminary days—a gifted pastor who had distinguished himself in the field of chancel drama. Without spending a lot time on small talk, he got into the subject that prompted his calling me and obviously was very heavy on him. He had been a pastor of St. John Lutheran Church in Gary, Indiana, a sort of mother church of Lutheranism in the area, housed in a high-towered, imposing, red brick structure with a two- story parochial school attached. In the last 18 months, the attendance at Sunday worship had plummeted. Reason: Whites have been moving out and

Negroes buying in. Rather than experience a Black invasion in the church, the congregation had chosen not to offer a Vacation Bible School that past summer.

He then said, "That's why I'm calling you, Karl. I just can't handle this situation. I'm accepting a call to a parish in Illinois. I know you have just taken on your new position at Valparaiso, but would you be able to serve St. John as vacancy pastor until they get a full-time pastor?"

I became immediately sad—sad for him because he really didn't want to run away from his flock, nor walk away from the shepherding challenge. And I felt sad for the congregation turning its back on people brought to them as neighbors with whom to share the graces God had given them.

My Sunday mornings had not yet been usurped by any other commitment so I agreed to being with the "survivors" on Sunday mornings, presiding at the Lord's Supper as well as bringing the Message of the Word—at least for a while.

Some weeks later, my wife Esther and I, together with a handful of St. John members who faithfully stayed, made house to house calls on a Sunday afternoon, telling their new neighbors, "Welcome! We're glad you're here!" But that's another story.

CHAPTER 3

FLASHBACK:
DECISION-MAKING AND MOVING

O ur congregation at the Lutheran Church of the Prince of Peace in Tulsa, Oklahoma, had always been very warm and supportive to Esther, our boys and me, as had the good people of Hope Church in Muskogee. So the encouragement of the Prince of Peace congregation that we go to Valparaiso University was very surprising.

In our meeting with the Tulsa people, it was emotionally difficult for them to make such a statement, but they were expressing their confidence that I would be able to serve God and God's people best in this new role of ministry at Valparaiso University. As years passed, Esther and I often reminded each other that we felt less "called" than "sent" as we found ourselves embarking on this turn in our life-journey.

Esther and I had had a strong reluctance to leave our fifteen-year ministry in Oklahoma. After examining and re-examining the pros and the cons of staying or leaving, we had agreed on the decision to decline, rather than accept, the position in Valparaiso. We surely did not wish to exclude the voices of our Prince of Peace members in our deliberations, so we scheduled a meeting to discuss the matter with these dear people.

That night, we met with our Tulsa congregation to share the letter proposing that we leave Oklahoma to take on the two-pronged post of ministry in Indiana. The document proposed that I teach on the University's Theology faculty, and become Field Secretary of the LHRAA. The mood of the members was sober and somber.

One after another, members of Prince of Peace congregation stood up and with deep emotion told how in their own experience, White Lutherans they had met revealed a serious need to face and change lingering attitudes of racial superiority and exclusiveness. They perceived the need for the church to take a strong stand against racism. We could hardly disagree and therefore found ourselves planning a move to Indiana.

I quickly discovered there was much more involved than merely taking on a new role in ministry. My decision to leave Oklahoma necessitated my withdrawing from a Tulsa Urban League assignment, which I had just recently accepted. I had also agreed to serve as voluntary chair of a committee to ensure quality housing for any residents who might be displaced in Tulsa's urban renewal program. The agenda before me was more than I had anticipated. Our leaving involved "closing shop" and tying up loose ends created by our moving.

The previous fall, the Oklahoma District had provided our congregation with an intern, Margaret Baden (Hansel) from Valparaiso University's Youth Leadership Training Program. Margaret performed valiantly, seeing to it that, in my leaving, the rhythm of the congregation's programs could be maintained without disruption of the church's ministries.

But then there was also the matter of packing books and files and such, finding a place to live, settling in at Valparaiso, beginning to ready myself for classroom responsibilities, and learning what my specific role would be as field secretary of the LHRAA. This made it necessary for me to precede the family northward and begin the house-hunting process as very soon as possible.

Add to the above a vast load of guilt because, in my going on ahead to Indiana, I was leaving Esther behind, with four young sons, and all the details that were now hers. Her immediate agenda called for uprooting the family, packing, and engaging the movers, plus dealing with the emotional strain of leaving behind a home, a host of precious friends, and readying herself for driving the boys and all the other last-minute items that could be squeezed into the car for the 800-mile journey. This was made even more difficult because Esther had recently had surgery.

The trip had a difficult start; it began with a flat tire only four blocks away from the home she was leaving. Our eighth grader, Peter, and his sixth-grade brother, Steve, had never before changed a tire, but now were enlisted to unpack the fully stuffed trunk to pull out the spare and try their hand at exchanging wheels so they once again could get on their way north.

I cannot recall all the details of what happened in those wild days. I do know when I boarded the plane and was trying to make sense out of all that was happening I was very, very tired. Once my flight ended in Chicago, I somehow got from the airport out to Park Forest—some fifty miles from Valpo. Our friends Ginny and Elmer Witt lived there and had agreed to drive me out to the University the next morning. I do remember Ginny taking one look at me and ushering me directly to a sofa where I stretched out and she massaged my back and shoulders until I fell asleep.

CHAPTER 4

NEW ROLE:
TEACHER AND PASTOR,
AND VERY MUCH STUDENT

I t was September, 1959, when I arrived on campus. Not much later, I was given the assignment to deliver the sermon in the main Sunday service in the awesome and majestic Memorial Chapel (later, given the name the Chapel of the Resurrection), which stretched out the length of a football field and reached six stories skyward. There were few more than a dozen of us who would be participating in leading the service. We'd been gathered in the small Gloria Christi Chapel, directly beneath the chancel of the large chapel. Some were student acolytes; others were faculty members who would assist with the various duties required for the occasion. Here is where we would receive and slip into the vestments we were to wear.

Robert Bertram, then Dean of the Chapel, orchestrated and supervised the operation. He led me to the side, reached up to a rod from which a string of stoles hung. He removed one and placed it across my shoulders. I was obviously excited. And as I noticed other clergy persons reaching up to take one of the several stoles still draped there, without thinking, I reached up to take one also and Bertram stopped me in my confusion, chiding me quickly with these words: "Remember the Scriptures, Karl: 'Let him that stoled, stole no more!'" His warm humor caused us all to chuckle and I relaxed a bit. But only a bit.

OP Kretzmann, Van Kussrow, and Karl Lutze
at the Chapel of the Resurrection

The swelling chords of the majestic organ, the carefully blended voices of the choir, and the robust singing of the hymns by the congregation of worshippers (about 2,000 at that time), my mounting the steps to the lofty pulpit—the grandeur of it all proved nearly overwhelming.

As the music ceased, the congregation spread out down below me rose to hear my reading from the Scriptures. Then, while I waited for the people to be seated again, my eyes wandered across the opened page of the large Bible before me. A small section of a verse in Psalm 119 came into focus: "I am very small." No other words could have been more appropriate.

So suddenly, I found myself accepting the role of teacher among a set of bright colleagues, who either had their doctorates or were pursuing them. It was most gratifying to experience the warm welcome they extended me. I felt no attitudes of condescension. On the contrary, already after my first year of teaching, my academic Dean, Dr. Alan Tuttle, invited me to his office. He commended me on the reports he had received, noting the effectiveness of my teaching. He offered me a financial incentive were I to choose to do graduate studies toward a doctorate. He made it quite clear, however, that maintaining my current status would not be jeopardized were I to decline his offer. He acknowledged the importance of my assignment to be working with LHRAA's program, especially at this critical moment of history.

A few years later, his successor, Dean Forrest Vance, stated his hopes that I would remain on the faculty roster without pursuing further degree enhancement. He noted that posting the list of faculty members and their academic achievements was intended to reflect the caliber of a university. So it would be advantageous to have as many people as possible on its roster who had a Ph.D. or its equivalent. Then he repeated "or its equivalent" and commented, "Your career certainly qualifies you as one having such equivalent."

Never condescending, ever encouraging, and deeply respecting the experiences in ministry and applied theology that I brought with me, all these colleagues welcomed me into their midst.

I was not really engaged as an "adjunct" member of the faculty. I participated in the Chapel's counseling program, and was regularly asked to speak both in the weekday chapel services and in Sunday morning worship services. I also attended all of our many (frequently twice-weekly!) department meetings. Our department Chair, Bob Bertram, once reminded us, "We may not always be 'all hailed fellows' but surely no one can accuse us of not being 'well met!'"

At the time, Valparaiso's Theology Department was introducing a unique curriculum requiring students to take a course in Theology in each of their first five semesters.

This curriculum, requiring students to write and submit an essay each week, imposed a rigid discipline on students taking these courses, but also provided opportunity for lively discussions among fellow students outside the actual classroom experiences. These essays were intended to provide them with an occasion to tie together material garnered from assigned readings with items discussed in class sessions. Of course, reading and grading ninety essays each week was no small task for the teacher. However, this facet of the program made it possible to know the students well. It opened the door to many visits with the students as they struggled with personal responses to religious issues to which they'd not previously given serious thought or been offered an opportunity to articulate.

It was the responsibility of the teaching staff to develop course content and to provide students with resources that were academically and personally challenging. The courses required the students' examination of Biblical and religious materials and their relevance to the lives of people of the past, our contemporaries, and our tomorrows. I was, of course, expected to participate in this enterprise. I could not have arrived at the University at a more favorable, challenging, or more exciting time.

At that time, more than 65 percent of the University's nearly 4,000 students were Lutheran. Presumably most of these in their earlier days back in their home churches had become acquainted with "the readings for the day" for the "church year." Using these texts to launch their studies, students were guided to probe their significance for life in historic times and in contemporary situations.

And the students! I was to teach three classes of thirty, meeting each class two times a week—all fresh from high schools all over the country, all filled with uncertain and wary excitement as was the neophyte teacher who faced them. And there'd be ninety essays they'd submit each week for me to read and to grade.

Rather than finding myself only as teacher, I more and more came to realize and enjoy my role of learner from these young scholars.

Likewise, the many, many times I would be sitting in our less-than-impressive and overcrowded office, with Dr. Schulze, proved to be for both of us a continuing learning process, an "occasion" for growing, insight, and sharing our "aha's."

Immersed in his ministry, Andrew worked long hours in long days with tireless enthusiasm. The "Institutes" he had developed proved to be both a rewarding affirmation of his life mission and an inspiring incentive to me to pursue and expand his efforts. I couldn't possibly have found or chosen a better partner, colleague in ministry, wise mentor, and genuine friend to help me fit into my new role. There were not enough hours in a day to allow for a lengthy and in-depth preparation for each day's work, either in the classroom or in our human relations responsibilities. There was too much that needed to be done—and done immediately.

St. Matthew, the Gospel writer, speaks of a situation that seems very close to matching my own as I took on my new post, moving from Oklahoma to Indiana. He quotes excerpts from Jesus' famous Sermon on the Mount, elaborating briefly on the theme: "No man can serve two masters."

I had agreed to serve two employers: VU – as a teacher; LHRAA – as a resource to the larger church community in its efforts to deal with race relations.

Each month, each of my two employers paid me the same amount as wages for my service. Although neither of these employers ever expressed dissatisfaction or doubt about my loyalty in my serving, I repeatedly found myself asking myself whether I was favoring one or the other.

I eventually succeeded in shaking off such fretting about the matter, once I designed my own self-scrutiny of the service record. Over a four-month span, I would select four "typical" weeks in which I would (as precisely as possible) mark off areas of my calendar/journal, time of my beginning some university work and ending as well as my resuming or starting some LHRAA duties.

This, of course, became tedious and nearly impossible as I might be engaged in writing an essay for the *VANGUARD* when I'd be interrupted by a student or university colleague working her way through some spiritual or theological struggles.

When I read and calculated the totals of my journal entries, I was surprised to learn that in the four weeks of my findings, I had been spending a minimum of thirty-five hours for each of the areas of service I was trying to assess.

But what about that Sermon on the Mount passage? It didn't take me too long to reflect—and to do some rationalizing—to realize that I was in the happy position of recognizing that my Master was not either one of those organizations. In both instances, I would find myself reflecting on the hymn stanza: "Let none but Christ your Master be."

And that's enough.

As LHRAA grew, the office added five staff persons. It was then that Andrew and Margaret Schulze were given a brief recess from all their responsibilities at our Valpo office, freeing them to attend sessions of the Lutheran World Federation gathering in Helsinki, Finland. They returned to the States on time to participate in the 1963 March on Washington, attended by over 250,000 participants from all over the country.

CHAPTER 5
VALPARAISO UNIVERSITY GROWS AND CHANGES

B y the time I arrived in Valparaiso, Andrew had already been on the scene for three years. The problems and challenges of unresolved Black/ White racial tensions in our country continued to surface, even after slavery had long been officially abolished. States in the South, however, legally enforced segregation on African-Americans until May 17th, 1954. On that day, the Supreme Court of the United States declared in the Brown vs. Board of Education decision, that segregation in public schools was no longer to be imposed in local communities across the country. "Separate but equal" was no longer acceptable at any level. Nonetheless, in the North, the habits of racial segregation were also evident almost everywhere, even without legal enforcement.

In the mid 1950s, Valparaiso University students Carolyn Roberts (Shephard) and Lou Jeanne Bray (Walton) were among the first few African-Americans to enroll at Valparaiso University. These two became roommates.

In my early days of ministry, Carolyn had been a member of my church, Hope Lutheran Church in Muskogee. I'd met Lou Jean when she was still a small child, and had come along with her parents from Pittsburgh to

Prof. Lou Jean Walton

attend our Summer Institute at Valparaiso. In later years, Lou Jean became a colleague of mine when she headed the Social Work Department at the University.

Their early experiences were trying. In Valparaiso, though allowed to shop in the local department store, they were not permitted to try on hats; when they approached the altar to receive the sacrament at Immanuel Lutheran Church in downtown Valparaiso (where students regularly attended Sunday worship), they noticed some people rise and leave the church. As late as the mid-1960s, no real estate agent in Valparaiso would sell property to any Black citizen.

In the early 1960s, Professor Jeff Johnson was the first full-time faculty member of color, Because of this community dynamic, he was provided with housing in a campus residence hall. He had been the first African-American to graduate from Concordia Seminary in St. Louis. He continued his graduate studies to receive a doctorate and became head of Valparaiso University's Department of Sociology, and, incidentally the first African-American resident of the city of Valparaiso.

By specific order, President Kretzmann informed those responsible for scheduling worship arrangements at the University's Chapel to make certain that Dr. Johnson would frequently be at the altar, serving as presiding minister at Sunday morning Holy Communion services.

Kretzmann was eager for such prominent visible positioning of African Americans, thereby making a clear and strong statement about the university's high respect for people of color.

CHAPTER 6

THE VALPARAISO UNIVERSITY/
MILES COLLEGE EXCHANGE

W
hen I answered the phone on a snowy, cold Indiana morning in the winter of 1964-65, I hardly expected to be talking with the President of the University. He told me he'd been reading about colleges and universities in the North that had launched exchange programs with schools on the roster of the 32-member United Negro College Fund. He asked that I explore possibilities for Valparaiso's connecting with such a southern Black school that was not yet involved in that kind of program.

I discovered quickly that schools like Talladega, Grambling, Shaw, Fisk, and others with whose names I was more familiar, had already been partnered with northern institutions, but a conversation with my long-time Alabama friend, Pastor Joe Ellwanger, put me on a track for exploring possibilities for establishing ties with Miles College, a small CME (Christian Methodist Episcopal) school in Birmingham.

Earlier, he had passed on to me a film released for the television series, *CBS Reports*, featuring anchor newsman Howard K. Smith. The show was called *Who Speaks for Birmingham?* One of the segments of the production focused on Dr. Lucius Pitts, the President of Miles College.

In viewing that brief clip, I had been tremendously impressed by this man, his comments, and his vision. He'd been filmed sitting alone in a middle seat of the otherwise empty Miles auditorium. There he unfolded his hopes for the role his underfunded, academically unaccredited, underequipped enterprise might fill to meet the challenges that lay before him and his colleagues. They had chosen to provide the best education possible for a student body of young African-Americans wanting to reach their fullest potential for leadership in a day when the heavy clouds of segregation, discrimination, and exclusion threatened their future.

I called President Pitts' office. The call revealed his excitement for exploring ways of carrying out this project of sharing. The many hurdles to be encountered in such a venture were immediately apparent. He was eager to study with me what establishing such a partnership would entail and what the program might look like if developed.

My first trip to Miles brought me to Birmingham late in the night. Dr. Pitts was at the airport to meet my flight and we drove directly to the college campus. My host briefed me a bit about Miles on the way.

As we arrived, our headlights flashed against the tall chain-link fence that surrounded the campus. Its gate was closed, attended by the watchman who had been sitting there on a metal folding chair, a rifle resting across his legs. As we turned in towards the gate, he rose from his seat. Upon recognizing the president's car, he greeted us briefly and unlocked the gate. Once we were inside, he locked the gate and resumed his post as watchman.

It was about 10:30 when we entered his home, located inside a corner of the fenced campus. Mrs. Pitts had not felt well, he told me, and had retired early. He was correct in his assumption that I would not have eaten. He promptly began to broil steaks for us and, as we dined, he continued to apprise me of the challenges he and his colleagues and students faced in the tense setting of the die-hard, vicious grip of the segregation manifest in Alabama.

As we ate and talked, he appeared troubled. He began glancing furtively toward the window and a large lawn that was illuminated by a strong flood light. He explained his anxiety: he had been noticing, beyond the fence, some car lights that seemed to leave and then return, then leave again, only to return. The week before, he explained, someone had thrown a piece of pipe over the fence into his yard. The police had come and removed it. Although he'd not yet received any subsequent official report, he assumed the pipe had been a bomb. This explained his wariness.

The next morning, my host took me to the administration building, where he introduced me to some of Miles' faculty members. Together, we initiated plans for a student exchange program between their school and Valparaiso University.

While components of a full-blown exchange program between our two schools called for more detailed planning, we agreed that a less formal initial attempt to effect ties might be workable. Without imposing responsibilities on Miles College for initial exploration, we agreed that we might, during the ensuing spring break, invite some VU students to sign up for a visit to Birmingham, anticipating a sort of trial run for the actual exchange.

Meanwhile, the early reports about the venture engendered excitement on our Valparaiso campus. Learning that in the school's pursuit of accreditation, Miles' library had need for more books, Valpo students—and faculty members, too—began a project to collect books to be sent to the Birmingham College.

It was not difficult to recruit Valpo students for an exploratory visit to Birmingham. This would allow us to anticipate problems and to maximize opportunities for the most effective implementation of our plan for the formal exchange between the two schools.

Since no university funds had been budgeted for this project, Valparaiso students paid their own way, contributing their own money to make possible the chartering of a bus and meeting other basic tour expenses. Even this limited exploration visit called for careful planning.

Dr. Pitts, Pastor Ellwanger, and I agreed to draw up a calendar of activities for the Valpo students' time in Alabama. The program called largely for meeting with community figures, Black as well as White, who would discuss with our students their own experiences as residents of Birmingham. Our hope was that they would share their perspectives of the local racial scene.

Dr. Lucius Pitt s (L) and Pastor Joe Ellwanger (R) plan gift for Miles College.

The courses would include lectures by people who were deeply involved in the Black/White issues. Among those engaged were the editor of Birmingham's Black newspaper; presidents of two church-related White colleges; two Black pastors active in civil rights, and two White clergy who were staunch supporters of George Wallace, the outspoken segregationist Governor of Alabama. The Valparaiso visitors would also spend one evening in a church crowded with Black citizens who would gather each week for mutual support as Birmingham Human Rights Organization with the renowned Black churchman, the Reverend Fred Shuttlesworth, presiding.

Miles College President Pitts and visiting VU students in Birmingham.

And students would also spend the larger part of an afternoon with a church-going Black entrepreneur, a Mr. A.G. Gaston, who through the years had become a millionaire. He was a mortician, a real estate agent, and a banker. All this followed his beginnings as a laborer in the steel mills. Mr. Chris McNair, father of Denise, one of the four little girls killed in the bombing of Birmingham's 16th Street Baptist Church, also agreed to share two hours in dialog with the students.

Dr. Pitts would also make room in his busy schedule for a lengthy session with students, sharing his perspective on his own experiences and telling of his dreams and plans for his school's future. Of course, there would be a session in which Miles students and Valpo students might share their ideas about preparing college students for meaningful roles in today's and tomorrow's world.

Again, Pastor Ellwanger was of inestimable help in constructing a workable experience for the visitors from the North. He arranged a "Volunteers Day," in which we'd be joining members of his St. Paul Lutheran Congregation, a church in the Black community served by this White pastor. We would be participating with members of St. Paul in the task of repainting their church building. Another feature of the program would assure possibilities for Valpo students to spend time with Miles students and, also to pair off with them in visiting African-American homes near the college, urging local residents to register for voting.

Meanwhile, VU professors Marc Riedel, Elspeth Loeppert, and Jeff Johnson agreed to serve as resource faculty personnel, escorting our students on the trip. They also paid their own ways. Lodging for women participants would be with Birmingham hosts and since Miles had no dormitories, beds were set up in the gymnasium for our male students.

It was more difficult to set up the "exchange" aspect of the project, which was to offer a partner course for the students from Miles. The primary problem: finances. There was absolutely no way that the Miles College administration, already operating on an austere budget, was able to afford any funds to support what Dr. Pitts and I wanted to be doing. Prospective participants from the Birmingham student body found themselves unable to purchase the twelve books assigned for the semester's readings, much less pay for their travel costs on a trip to Indiana.

Although Valparaiso University's finances were already strained, the President's office and the Business staff made it possible for us to structure and offer a course at Miles called "The Church and Race—North." This contribution, plus a modest donation from the VU Student Senate, made it possible to purchase the needed books and to underwrite the travel costs of Miles College participants. I was to be in Birmingham to lecture and launch the course at Miles the first five days of the spring semester. Thereafter, the class would meet with a Miles faculty member two hours each week to discuss the assigned readings.

Upon my return to Valpo, following this "trial run," we would be prepared to launch the more polished program. This called for me to be the instructor of a class offered at Valparaiso University entitled "The Church and Race – South."

Between the beginning of the spring semester and the Easter recess, participating Valparaiso students would be required to read the twelve books. Every two weeks, they'd meet in two-and-a-half hour sessions to discuss with their classmates and me the books they'd been reading. Meanwhile, in Birmingham, the students who had enrolled in the parallel course, "The Church and Race – North" were meeting in the same way with a Miles Religion professor.

During the Miles spring break, this same Miles professor accompanied the students on their trip to Indiana. The aim of this week-long visit was to provide them with the experience of meeting people involved in church life in the North, particularly in the context of interracial patterns as the social culture of this northern study would unfold.

During one of these sessions at Valparaiso, one student told of a letter he had received that week from his mother, a member of a rather large Baptist church in Chicago. She wrote that the previous Sunday her pastor, in his sermon, had mentioned a visit at his office with Scott Umbreit, a young member of the congregation enrolled in Valparaiso University (and in my class). He told his pastor how in class discussions he'd been assigned to read for a class: *The Autobiography of Malcolm X*. My student had spoken so excitedly about the book that the pastor had himself purchased a copy and read it. He too had found the book so moving that he urged those present for his sermon to read the book too. It was affirming to me that the work we were doing with students like Scott was spreading beyond the classroom.

On our campus, the Miles students met with now past-president, Chancellor Kretzmann, President Huegli, (his successor), Dean of the Chapel Nagel and a few faculty members, as well as Professor Jeff Johnson.

On side trips to Chicago, the Miles students spent a morning participating in Jesse Jackson's Operation Breadbasket. They also interviewed inner city parish workers (Protestant, Roman Catholic, both White and African-American), as well as those serving suburban parishes.

Their schedules also included visits to the Interdenominational Urban Training Center for Christian Mission. There, pastors and other church workers enrolled in special courses that prepared them to understand and respond to the dynamic complexities of overcrowded metropolitan areas. The churches, their pastors, and their leaders had found themselves to be inexperienced and unready to respond to the situations confronting them and in many cases, were fearful of inherent challenges to the churches.

In Gary, they had conversations with Mayor Richard Hatcher, graduate of Valparaiso University School of Law and Gary's first African-American Mayor. They also met with Rev. Norman Brandt, White pastor of the self-supporting, heavily African-American membership, St. John Lutheran Church. His was the oldest Lutheran parish in Gary. Most of its White membership had moved to suburban neighborhoods, joining churches there.

Courses in both schools provided opportunities for students of Miles and Valpo to be with one another and to share their thoughts about their experiences in each other's situation—North and South.

The exchange program proved rewarding for all who participated. The students actually enrolled in the experience, guest lecturers, all those who assisted in planning the program, expressed enthusiastic and favorable reviews of their involvement.

But after our third time around, in spite of its favorable reception, in spite of all its benefits, the program's demands on my schedule and the dollars and cents costs exceeded the resources necessary to justify its continuance. The Miles course was still offered at VU's campus, minus the personal confrontation with racial issues that had been built into the original Miles curriculum.

When I got to Miles College with the practice run, to my surprise, one of the participants was my eldest son, Peter Charles Lutze. And then I found it gratifying that Peter had signed up for the first full session as well.

CHAPTER 7

THESE PROVE TO BE MY TUTORS

A ndrew Schultze's first assignment for me when I arrived in 1959 on the LHRAA scene was to draw up plans for the 1960 Human Relations Institute. The pattern for these summer gatherings clearly had been well developed through their brief but eminently successful history. The ingredients of these three-day meetings included theological presentations by Lutheran scholars. Students and scholars would explore with institute participants scriptural mandates and guidelines for responding to the challenges presented by the racial disparities that were becoming more and more apparent in world happenings.

Another piece of each year's Institute's agenda allowed an opportunity for Institute participants to share their experiences in dealing with problems encountered in their congregations or neighborhoods "back home." It was equally important that they were provided an opportunity to engage in conversation with others who attended, exchanging encouraging stories of their successful efforts to find allies in the task of breaking down and ending these segregating institutions.

Perhaps the most unusual feature of the Institutes was the presentation of a major essayist—almost always a non-Lutheran speaker who would examine with the audience aspects of the racial issue from different perspectives. This, in itself, was unique because most Lutheran gatherings rarely invited people of other denominations to present their experiences and perspectives in a formal instructional role.

I found that these Institute guest speakers became tutors of mine as well, not only in their formal presentations to the Institute audiences, but also in spending time with them in personal conversation during their stay on campus and later in personal correspondence. It was as if we were engaging in a one-on-one seminar as they made indelible impressions on my eager-to-learn-from-them mind.

KYLE HAZELDEN, prior to his becoming editor of *The Christian Century*, had served as White pastor of an all-White American Baptist congregation in the South (Charleston, West Virginia). It was then that he had authored his book, *The Racial Problem in Christian Perspective*. Although I knew him through his writings, I had never met him until he accepted our invitation to address the 1963 Summer Institute on campus.

A few years later, when Cleveland Lutheran churches and their pastors called on LHRAA to help them respond to the explosive racial outbursts there, I urged them to seek also the counsel of Dr. Hazelden. Since I was able to be present at his Cleveland interaction with the churches, this gave me more opportunity to know and to learn from this gifted man. In months that followed, I utilized as a classroom text, the superb book mentioned above. His contribution—and my conversations with him—informed and confirmed much of what was the central concern of my own ministry.

In essence, Hazelden called on churches and their leaders to realize that our role, in days of social disruption, was to be more than that of passive observer and dispenser of a sedative message that benumbs. Sadly, that message often has served to justify disinterest in its audience and encourage non-involvement. Hazelden saw his role as trumpeter, as a wake-up call to the Church that has actually been a key—albeit unwilling—player in the tragic, explosive rioting that had erupted in so many cities. He cited the churches and their members as "Mother of Racial Patterns, Purveyor of Arrant Sedatives, and Teacher of Immoral Moralities."

Hazeldon identified three core aspects of racial prejudice that Whites should recognize:

1. Discrimination—discernible in denying any other person the Right to Have;

2. Segregation—denying another person the Right to Belong; and

3. Stereotyping—denying the victim the Right to Be.

For Christians to practice or condone any of these three would be unthinkable.

 **JAMES MCBRIDE DABBS**, college professor, life-long southern gentleman, conscientious Christian layman, and prolific author, was president of the South Carolina Council on Human Relations at the time he addressed the Valparaiso Institute on Human Relations in July, 1963. An impressive figure—tall, kindly, thoughtful, courageous and, though clearly a spokesman on behalf of desegregation—much respected by his South Carolina segregationist neighbors for his personal integrity.

I learned from him how to search for and to discern the consistent, simultaneous presence of two inherent and underlying structures: one of these is life nurturing, a structure of grace and goodness; the other, its opposite is a structure of destruction, of evil, and ultimately proves deadly.

These dynamics are complex and may have unintended consequences. They are neither easy nor simple. For example, when we engage in acts or programs of kindness and generosity, a latent, selfish, and prideful desire for recognition may surface. Or we may find ourselves justifying our ignoring of the needy and/or endorsing and participating in actions that may hurt others, our environment, or constructive relations among people.

Conversely, when we see people whose lives have been diminished by brutal action or by thoughtless neglect, the situation may evoke a sensitive and caring response. Participation in beautifying a disheveled and shoddy neighborhood block might prompt a 'clean-the-city program.' This project could uproot the aging widow whose tired little house is to be demolished. It is not simply another version of the folksy cliché: 'behind every gray cloud there's a silver lining.' These powerful dynamics required thoughtful, critical reflection and the development of strategies that would lessen the down side (like finding a satisfactory home for the aging widow) if the overall good was sufficiently strong and the negative consequences could be addressed.

Some months after the Institute where we had first met Dr. Dabbs, Esther and I were guests of LHRAA North Carolina's board members, Dr. Bob and Caroline Miller, at their home in Charlotte. They suggested driving down to visit the Rip Rock Plantation in South Carolina where Professor James Dabbs lived.

With the help of directions provided by some of his neighbors, we found our way to a sandy boulevard lined by a stately row of trees that wound into a circle in front of the porch of an imposing mansion. Doubtless, it had once been a jewel on the landscape, but it was now in a rather sorry state of disrepair.

The white-haired gentleman, with Mrs. Dabbs at his side, stepped down the stairs to welcome us. He issued a quick sort of apology for the somewhat shabby appearance of the great house, "If any of the people down here should have a spruced-up domicile, the neighbors might well assume that the owner had really not fully supported the South in the War of the States."

As he ushered us into the spacious living room, his wife disappeared into the kitchen to prepare some cold lemonade for us. Above the fireplace hung two Civil War muskets; one across the other. Beneath, standing on the mantle, was a large golden plaque mounted on a piece of polished oak wood. Bright sunlight reflecting on the brass metal made it difficult to read, so I stepped closer in order to study its message:

In Recognition of his Outstanding Contribution
to the Cause of Improved Race Relations
in our Country,
the NAACP of Detroit, Michigan, Commends
Dr. James McBride Dabbs
for his Extremely Faithful Service.

And we wondered how South Carolina neighbors visiting the Dabbs home might have responded to that impressive citation mounted there.

His gift to me? He was a vivid role model who lived an unflinching, uncompromising commitment to a dual path of championing the cause of Blacks in their efforts to

THESE PROVE TO BE MY TUTORS

capture their rightful status as fully human children of God, free to develop and to exercise their place in God's world and in this country. Simultaneously, he would be reaching out to fellow southern Whites trapped in a deeply imbedded segregationist culture and lifestyle. While many voices in pulpits of southern churches were reluctant—and often fearful—Jim courageously pointed to the full implications and relevance of the Gospel and of the biblical imperative that we love our neighbor.

Similarly, **WILL CAMPBELL**, another life-long White southerner, agreed to address our Institute family in 1967. He, unlike James Dabbs, however, came with experience as a clergyman. Will, a brilliant writer, was also an engaging speaker. His folksy style at once both charmed and disturbed those in his audience who either subtly or blatantly supported the segregating attitudes and practices that marked so many aspects of life in the South.

For a while, Campbell had served as a Director of Spiritual Care at the University of Mississippi. In that capacity, Will had invited an African-American chaplain serving a nearby military post to visit him in his office. When his guest arrived on campus, Will walked with him to the faculty room. A ping-pong table was there and Will challenged his guest to a game. Later in the day, after the chaplain had left, Will received a message: he was to report to the president's office at once. He went there immediately and was told that reports had been received citing the incident in the faculty room. In sharp reprimand, Will was asked, hadn't he realized "this is the South and this is a state institution?"

Will responded—and one could readily imagine the feigned look of innocence that must have crossed his face as he spoke. He defended himself and appealed to the South's insistence that gatherings of White people and African-Americans were always to be subject to the rule supporting the segregation of Whites and Blacks: Separate but Equal.

Will explained, "Well, we were at a ping-pong table; there was a net between us and each had separate but equal paddles and each of us had an equal-sized half of the table on which to play." There was no need for further conversation. Will Campbell was dismissed from his position at the University and he moved on to become the Associate Executive Director, Department of Racial and Cultural Relations of the National Council of Churches.

GEORGE KELSEY, a professor at Drew University School of Theology in Madison, New Jersey, was one of the Institute speakers. Insights he shared at the Institutes in 1966 and 1968 I still find meaningful today.

"God created man in his own image; and immediately man would return the favor, and recreate God in man's image, determined to exalt the creature and dethrone God the Creator. The fall of Adam means separation, separation from God, alienation, hostility, because man insists on taking God's place. . .

" . . . The churches have the responsibility to repudiate the notion, to which they have contributed, that there is any aspect or area of life that does not fall under the Lordship of Christ. Churchmen must stop going around announcing that the powers that be are ordained of God and then permitting them to rule by expediency and reasons of state. If the powers that be are ordained of God, then the powers that be are subject to the Law of God, and the prophets of the Lord must proclaim this and continue to proclaim it."

WILLIAM STRINGFELLOW first came to our attention when we received an envelope in the campus mail from the University's President, Dr. O.P. Kretzmann. He enclosed some pages from *The Christian Century* that featured an article by Stringfellow, together with O.P.'s own comments penned in the margin: "Watch for this young man's writings. He has important things to say and does so well."

Upon graduation from Harvard Law School, Bill had set up his office in New York City's Harlem, specifically to be a lawyer for the poor. Some described the site where he planted himself as the ugliest block in the country—crowded, abject poverty at every turn, high crime, miserable housing, outrageous sanitation conditions, inadequate health service, rodent infestation and more. This was where the young, White, newly-minted lawyer chose to establish his work.

In his writings, as well as in his addresses, Stringfellow's message insisted on helping the Christian individual—as well as the larger Christian community—recognize the choices we always face—either good or evil. Each situation demands making a choice between either good or evil, ultimately the choice between life and death. "There is no option to be 'not' involved. But we are not to be conformed—constrained. Even the decision not to be involved—or to be silent, or to withdraw—or to endorse inaction, neglect, or silence is to join forces with death dealing movements and actions."

Twice Bill accepted our invitations to address our Human Relations Institutes on campus. He was first with us in 1965. He was an excellent, engaging speaker. He was a member of the Episcopal Church and people hearing him would often comment on his theological prowess. While he did admit to reading in the Scriptures every day, he did not like to be introduced as a "lay theologian." He was eager to distance himself from any academic study of theology, wanting to present his convictions as essential to a Christian expression of loyalty to the teachings of his faith in Christ.

The last time I was with Stringfellow occurred after he'd come to Valparaiso to present an address on our campus. It was on that occasion I became aware of the intensity of his deteriorating physical condition.

Prior to accepting our invitation, he had already apprised us of his failing health. Because he could only digest a small amount of food at a time, he had to have frequent, small amounts of food. If he were to be deprived of food for more than even a very short time, the situation might well assume life-threatening dimensions.

I had assured him that I would personally be his chauffeur to avoid any such happening. So once he had finished his presentation, I drove my car to the hall where he'd been speaking and we were immediately ready to get on our way to O'Hare Airport, Chicago, normally a trip of no more than two hours. After only a few miles, we were relieved to find ourselves already on the Interstate.

I recall vividly how, even as we found ourselves in deep conversation, we also suddenly had found ourselves in deep traffic. The three lanes on our side of the concrete median were packed with cars and we had been slowed to a crawl. Flashing red and blue lights and screaming sirens were accompanied by patrol cars, ambulances and emergency vehicles racing down the shoulders on our right. The sea of cars all around us had come to a complete halt.

Some of the frustrated drivers stepped from their cars, attempting to view the cause of the disruption. Although we had no way of knowing the cause of this gridlock, it was obvious that we in no way were going to find a quick, easy, and immediate escape. We'd become captive to the snarled traffic. No sign announcing an exit ramp was anywhere in sight. No space was available in lanes either to our left or right, even had there been, our highway had become a virtual over-crowded parking lot. I was ever so grateful that we had allotted ample time to provide a margin of at least two hours before we needed to be at the airport for flight check-in.

With all the emergency help on hand to attend to the cause of the tie-up, we comforted ourselves, agreeing that things surely would soon be moving once again.

Meanwhile, in the midst of all this, here I was in personal conversation with William Stringfellow, whom I had come to respect as one of the most brilliant minds, clearest thinkers, most eloquent writers, most dedicated Christians I had ever been privileged to meet.

I plied him with question after question and he generously responded with a sharing of his life stories, experiences, his faith, and many more moments of his very productive life.

When I asked Bill about his present activities, he told me of his home in Rhode Island. A most recent house guest there had been the Reverend Daniel Berrigan, the Jesuit priest whose name had become widespread because of his activist role as protester opposed to the Vietnam War.

Father Berrigan, together with a renowned political scientist, Howard Zinn, had traveled to Hanoi and actually succeeded in persuading the North Vietnamese army to release three American prisoners of war. This, of course, won Father Berrigan great respect and he, together with eight others (they became known as the Catonsville Nine) broke into a government office in the Baltimore suburb of Catonsville, Maryland, seized official files of draft information, removed 378 draft files, poured blood on them to express the deadliness of the war, then set fire to the files as symbol of the weapon of fiery napalm used in the war to kill people by flame.

A warrant had been issued against the priest who then chose to elude the FBI, to the chagrin and frustration of the FBI's notorious J. Edgar Hoover.

Berrigan found that countless allies were ready to enlist as his supporters. Repeatedly, Sunday after Sunday, Berrigan would show up at different churches by invitation of the local priest. There, he would speak on behalf of a Christian posture against war. By the time the report on his presence would reach the officers of the law and they would arrive at the scene, the elusive priest's friends would already have whisked him away to some sheltered and unannounced location. It was at this point that Father Berrigan was provided with safe harbor at Bill Stringfellow's Rhode Island home.

One foggy and chill Sunday morning, while the ubiquitous priest was Bill's houseguest, FBI agents arrived on the scene. The waters to the Island had been exceptionally riled, Bill observed. He could imagine that half of the men must surely have been seasick as they cruised the wild waves. They arrived in the guise of bird watchers, binoculars and all. As this "posse" swooped down on Stringfellow's home, they were sure that they had successfully tracked down their fleeing fugitive. The actual capturing proved less than a jubilant or triumphant showdown as they accosted him leisurely walking down the road to greet them.

The neighbors, intent on not having themselves or Stringfellow seen as harboring a fugitive, told the arresting officers that they had no part in concealing the visitor's presence nor had Bill Stringfellow. They claimed that they had regularly seen Father Berrigan each day walking down to the local post office to get the mail. And that was how, at long last, the "law" finally got their man.

Bill chuckled as he told his story. And there were more.

By now, however, much more time had elapsed and traffic remained at a standstill. I sensed a growing anxiety in my passenger and I became aware that I, too, was beginning to experience feelings of nervous uncertainty. Suddenly, but slowly, all the lanes of traffic, as if gently nudged, began to roll slowly ahead. The pace resembled a funeral procession. Then with low voice, Bill, almost in desperation, said, "Karl, I need food!"

I signaled to claim the lane to my right and tapped my horn. Somehow, the driver next to me caught my urgency, slowed his car and made space for mine. To my astonishment, some thirty yards ahead, off the road's shoulder on the right, an exit ramp opened, inviting me out of the entanglement. And only two or three blocks farther, a small grocery appeared. Unwilling to use up any of his waning strength, Bill whispered, "Buy a banana!"

I did. We resumed our travel. He ate the fruit. He caught his flight. And I returned to Valpo.

* * * * *

There were no quick and easy answers for the problems LHRAA was endeavoring to deal with. Those pastors and parishes who were reluctant to speak out against the exclusive conduct of their ministry did not appreciate the insistence on taking seriously the urging of St. Paul in his letter to the Romans, "Therefore welcome one another as Christ has welcomed you, for the glory of God."

The churches of the 1960s, in the North as well as the South, seemed rather disposed to turn away from such mandates of Scripture. This seemed to be particularly the case as pastors and lay leaders refused to abandon any vestige or pattern that tolerated or defended segregation.

On one morning, as he opened mail that had come to our office, Andrew paused to read aloud to me a letter from two apparently seasoned southern Lutheran women, who informed us that they had reported our 'irresponsible and persistent censure of the segregated way of life' to Senator James Eastland. This congressman was notoriously and vociferously supportive of segregation.

Senator Eastland went so far as to post Andrew's and my name on the House Un-American Activities list. With this list he was naming and accusing people whose speech and conduct was interpreted by him to be exposing their un-American leanings and commitments. This list was given to the FBI as suspected communists.

Eastland was so committed to segregation that he told President Lyndon Johnson that the recent lynching of three civil rights workers (Andrew Goodman, James Chaney, and Michael Schwerner) in Mississippi was a hoax. He dismissed it as "a publicity stunt and they were probably in Chicago."

Because those persons included on that list were regarded as un-American and Communist, LHRAA invited FBI head J. Edgar Hoover to address our Summer Institute and warn people against the hasty condemning of others about such unpatriotism. He declined our invitation and assigned his number-one assistant, William Sullivan, to address the following year's LHRAA Institute at Valpo.

Sullivan did indeed accept our invitation, giving what some of us regarded as a bland presentation, which did however, remove the issue of LHRAA being communists from the minds of some of our critics.

But there were still Lutherans who were not happy with LHRRA's ministry.

At the time parochial schools in the South were recruiting children of White parents who were looking for ways to circumvent the desegregation of public schools. They were sending their children to Lutheran schools that had no Black children enrolled. A pastor in Tennessee wrote a letter to our LHRAA office, reprimanding me for an article I had written, criticizing churches that opened their parish school doors to people trying to resist the Supreme Court decision ordering public schools to eliminate segregation. He accused us of blocking his church's attempt to win families for church membership. And furthermore, he saw our position as hurting the financial benefits the school would enjoy from a new source of revenue for undergirding the church's overall programs.

CHAPTER 8

CHARTING A COURSE—
WIDESPREAD DISRUPTIONS DETERMINED
LHRAA'S AGENDA

R eflecting on the days of World War II, when factories in northern states were operating around the clock in the manufacture of materials needed for military use, it was clear that the demand for more workers exceeded the number available. Employment doors opened wide.

As a result, increasingly women and African-Americans were sought to fill positions previously not accessible to them. Vast numbers of African-Americans migrated to northern industrial centers, often moving into already over-crowded housing areas.

Settled residents, local neighborhood businesses, and established churches were generally unprepared to accommodate, let alone reach out welcoming arms, to the newcomers. Social and cultural differences as well as latent prejudices resulted in chilled relationships, ugly confrontations, and in some instances, bitter clashes between newcomers and the longtime residents.

Schools, playgrounds, churches, and other institutions such as the YMCA and YWCA, (which had previously served to pull people of a community together, creating, fostering and maintaining an atmosphere of neighborliness) all proved ineffective in achieving such lofty goals.

Local congregations, national church bodies, and regional judicatories were also unprepared to deal with these issues. LHRAA was organized to respond actively to these struggles.

In 1954, a year after LHRAA's ministry was launched, ESCRU (*Episcopal Society for Cultural and Racial Unity*) came into being. The following year we became aware of the development of NCCRR (*National Catholic Conference on Religion and Race*), a voluntary association of Roman Catholics—lay and clergy. Subsequently, such organizations sprouted in other denominations: BARB: (*Baptist Anti-Racial Bias*), PIC (*Presbyterian Interracial Council*). In each instance, these seemed to be telling their respective denominations that eliminating racial exclusiveness deserved a place of high priority on the Church's agenda of problems to be addressed.

After Andrew Schulze's retirement in 1964, I became Executive Director of LHRAA. I attended a week-long workshop at the University of Wisconsin in Madison, in which the pattern for reflection followed a system developed by the renowned and respected Peter Drucker. It was called *Management by Objectives*. The program proved very helpful for me in providing a roadmap for the effective programming of LHRAA's ministry.

However, the agenda for LHRAA was largely set for us by the tumultuous and explosive social upheaval that was bursting in larger cities all over the country, where racial confrontations spread like contagion. As the National Commission on Civil Disorders March, 1968, also known as the *Kerner Report* (page 35, mid-page) observed:

> Between 1963 and 1964 . . . serious disorder involving both Whites and Negroes, broke out in Birmingham, Savannah, Cambridge, Maryland, Chicago, and Philadelphia. Sometimes the mobs battled each other; more often they fought the police.
>
> The most violent encounters took place in Birmingham. Police used dogs, fire hoses and cattle prods against marchers [protestors], many of whom were children. White racists shot at Negroes and bombed Negro residences. Negroes retaliated by burning White owned businesses in Negro areas. On a quiet Sunday morning a bomb exploded beneath a Negro church. Four young girls in a Sunday School class were killed. Civil rights demonstrators provoked violence in Jacksonville. A shot fired from a passing car killed a Negro woman. When a bomb threat forced evacuation of an All-Negro high school, students stoned policemen and firemen and burned the cars of newsmen. For the first time, Negroes used Molotov cocktails [homemade, gasoline-fueled bottles] in setting fires.
>
> Two weeks later at a demonstration protesting school segregation in Cleveland, a bulldozer accidentally killed a young White minister.
>
> When police moved in to disperse the crowd, composed primarily of Negroes, violence erupted.

In 1943 already there had been a fierce rioting in Detroit but now the violence emerges once again with viciousness. The list includes: "New York's Harlem, Brooklyn, Rochester, Jersey City, and Philadelphia.

In Spring of 1965 the nation's attention shifted back to the south . . . Selma, Alabama . . . Bogalusa, LA . . . forty-three disorders and riots were reported during 1966. Although there were considerable variations in circumstances, intensity, and length, they were usually ignited by a minor incident fueled by pent-up antagonism between the Negro population and the police.

Los Angeles. . . Thirty six hours after the first Guard units arrived, the main force of the riot had been blunted. Almost 4000 persons were arrested. Thirty-four were killed and hundreds injured. Approximately 35 million dollars in damage had been inflicted.

We, out in Valparaiso, were located only sixty minutes from Chicago, that metropolitan center which—at almost every level—had, for almost two decades been bulging with an influx of people migrating from the southern states. Multiple demoralizing issues faced the city: overcrowded housing; inadequate municipal services, understaffed schools in makeshift emergency trailer classrooms and rising drop-out numbers. There were in addition inadequate traffic control, distrust of police and public officials, and the emergence of gangs. All these factors and more contributed to making the city a center of tension and unrest.

There had been a day when neatly tended lawns and gardens and attractive homes had been the pride of the city. People, who saw the change coming to their neighborhood like an avalanche, readily blamed the arrival of these dark-skinned newcomers for their losses—of property value, of comfortable surroundings, of former gardens and attractive vistas.

A course I was teaching at VU as a theology offering was titled *The Church and the Racial Issue.* Chicago provided us with a situation where we could observe the problems resulting from the mass migration and the churches reaction to those situations.

We talked with pastors whose members had sold their homes to move to all-white suburban communities. We talked with pastors whose White congregations were exploring possibilities for merging with other nearby churches whose White membership was also declining even though they were members of other Lutheran church bodies.

During that semester, I required my students to attend a meeting of Operation Push in Chicago. Attending this meeting was a major culture challenge for my young students (who came from varied backgrounds and experiences) to be at this almost all Black meeting in the inner city.

I still remember that on several of the essays, submitted at the time, the student who was driving had warned his passengers he was locking his car doors now because they were entering the Black community. Understandable? Unnecessary?

For these students, the Saturday morning meetings of the largely Black audience presided over by the Reverend Jesse Jackson proved to be the most memorable learning experience in the course. I wanted them to observe, and participate in this meeting in order to get a religious perspective from Black people—churched or otherwise.

In this meeting, Reverend Jackson involved the audience in a sort of "call and response creed:"

He would say: "I may not have a decent home!" and the audience would repeat the phrase, "I MAY NOT HAVE A DECENT HOME!"

Jackson: "But I am somebody!"
Audience: "BUT I AM SOMEBODY!"
Jackson: "I may not have a decent job."
Audience: "I MAY NOT HAVE A DECENT JOB!"
Jackson: "But I am somebody!"
Audience "BUT I AM SOMEBODY!"
Jackson: "I may have spent time in jail."
Audience: "I MAY HAVE SPENT TIME IN JAIL!"
Jackson: "But I am somebody!"
Audience: "BUT I AM SOMEBODY!"

After five or six such statements he would say: I am God's child! And the people would shout, "I AM GOD'S CHILD!"

Following that meeting, the students were assigned to submit an essay presenting their emotional response to this event.

I don't recall how many of my students there were who participated in these Chicago visits and heard the strong message of Dr. Jesse Jackson. Now, years long after I laid my teaching tools aside, I still hear from former students words of appreciation for that experience.

This part of the course complemented reports I provided, describing the coalescing of ten leaders of the various regional and national Lutheran church bodies. This meeting had climaxed with their commitment to financially support LHRAA's engaging a director of an inner-city project. This project was designed to identify feasible programs for connecting workers and volunteers to discover ways of being involved and assisting as change agents. The combined financial investment made possible the purchase a building labeled the "Mansion."

This project, to be called LHRAA—Chicago Project, was not intended to be a new church. We engaged Pastor George Hrbek to be our project director. Some high school students, and college students as well, from miles around, were welcome to spend time in the community and nights at the Mansion. They brought in sleeping bags and were committed to study and serve. The impetus for participation was the Supper, the worship, and the serving. The enterprise was not the establishing of an organization, but a gathering of people finding useful engagement with other members of God's family to augment the caring aspect of Christ's ministry and welcome to all.

People—church, community and political leaders, bright lights in the industrial and commercial world, educators and news analysts—found no ready formulas to regain order and to discover ways of dealing constructively with the situation. No organized leadership seemed to be prepared and available to respond to such an enormous social disruption.

Some of the most urgent and pressing phone calls were coming to us from presidents (bishops) of regional sub-divisions of Lutheran churches requesting some specific service or assistance. Such contacts became useful doorways connecting us directly with congregations and pastors serving in neighborhoods where tensions were especially intense. We found them looking to us to interpret the situations facing them. They wanted guidance and suggestions of ways to respond to "their problem," not realizing that they themselves, in many cases, were a part of the problem.

They really wanted to avoid and remove "the problem" that lay at their churches' doorsteps. Radical voices weren't appearing only at commercial sites like restaurants to participate in sit-ins, on Sunday mornings they were even showing up in prominent churches for "kneel-ins."

The church folk were indeed aware that "there is a problem out there." We had to help them realize WE were a part of the problem. It was church people who, fearful of losing the value of their homes, brought pressure on real estate salespeople to "red-line" their neighborhoods, marking those places unavailable to Black buyers. It was people who had just paid off the mortgage on their new house of worship. They feared that welcoming new neighbors who were Black to their services would discourage other prospective White members, who wouldn't want their own teenagers in a youth program that "would attract and include colored kids." There were those who were reluctant to even have discussions on racial matters or on "Negro rights" in their adult Bible study groups.

Summers became the season of anxieties across the nation—especially in the 1960s—as riots broke out in overcrowded sections of major cities, especially in the metropolitan centers of the North and far West. Blazing buildings, clouds of tear gas, cracking rifle shots, national guard troops, screaming sirens of racing ambulances, military vehicles, shattered glass everywhere, defiant mobs in the streets, and the flashing lights of fire trucks and police cars. And people in all the big cities were waiting and wondering where will the next riot be—and when?

One of the more dramatic instances of LHRAA's direct involvement in this explosive atmosphere started with a phone call from some pastors in Cleveland. Some leaders from time to time would meet to discuss aspects of cooperative possibilities to serve the people of greater Cleveland. I was told there were nearly ninety-five clergy who would be invited to their sessions. This included district presidents, chaplains, and students from seminaries who were serving their internship periods in different congregations in the city. The person who called told of the violently explosive disruption that had occurred in Cleveland and asked whether I would meet with them and help them find a way for the churches to develop a strategy for responding to what had become a frightening issue.

I agreed to go to Cleveland and lead what would amount to a full morning session with the group. We arranged for an early-as-possible meeting that might produce a creative plan to meet the challenge confronting us. I led the meeting and brought with me two other professional churchmen whom I had come to know as particularly knowledgeable in understanding transracial problems. When I entered the church the men who were responsible for inviting the pastors informed me that they had expected an attendance of forty-five or fifty participants. Ninety had not only promised to attend, but were already present and eager for the meeting to start.

After the formal presentations were completed and discussed, enthusiasm was expressed about collaboration to study the possibilities and do so as very soon as possible. I suggested that it might be wise to engage someone to organize and orchestrate a program that would provide a realistic involvement of all the Lutheran churches in addressing the tense situation that so deeply threatened the city's well-being. I highly recommended they approach Pastor Richard Sering, an inner-city pastor in St. Louis, to see if he would work with the churches for three months in the summer. He accepted the position and immediately introduced programs which enjoyed an enthusiastic response of support by his sponsors. By

Pastor Richard Sering.

the end of the summer significant evidence of effective performance was noticeable and well received. But when Sering returned to St. Louis in the fall, the program lost its strength. The group asked him to return fulltime and become the Executive Director of what was now to be called LHRAA Cleveland. It quickly won the confidence of other pockets in the community and won financial support for its performance.

College and high school youth in many instances felt the churches of the day, their programs and their message were failing to address social and humane issues that marked the tensions that came with crowded cities and the problems of their people. The discussion of such matters seemed to be avoided in the programs and pulpits of the traditional churches.

We found an increasing number of young people, many of them Lutheran college students from Midwest schools wanting to become personally engaged in responding to the need for change in political, cultural, social and human inequities. As a result many of these young people were heading to the cities to volunteer in projects developed there. They often were unsure as to what they could do, but were looking for ways to be involved.

The English District (which was formed to serve non-German-speaking Lutherans), as well as the Northern Illinois District of the LCMS, in combined efforts to address human relations problems in Chicago's south side, asked LHRAA to propose ways of collaboration of leaders of those church groups to orchestrate a program to respond to their needs.

Those groups also provided financial support. LHRAA added a new position to our staff, engaging Pastor George Hrbek and assigning him to explore ways of meeting the tensions of the hour. This new structure would be known as LHRAA Chicago and would be quartered in a huge house that came to be known as "the Mansion." Students with sleeping bags would move in for the weekends, church

Pastor George Hrbek

services were conducted there and pastoral counseling help was a service offered.

As the need for such headquarters diminished, the building was remodeled. Years later, it became the residence of *President and Mrs. Barack Obama.*

However, LHRAA Chicago faced difficulties of church body collaboration and support for its ministerings. This problem resulted in Pastor Hrbek's moving to Cleveland and heading up a program there in the structure Pastor Sering had developed. It proved tremendously successful in rehabilitating ex-convicts. When Pastor Sering died after a lengthy siege of cancer, George Hrbek became his successor.

The Cleveland enterprise now had grants and other contributions providing support. It functioned quite separately from LHRAA and to this day is a well supported and an extremely effective servant in the Cleveland area under the title Lutheran Metropolitan Ministries.

During this tension of the 60's, an increasing number of individuals, mainly pastors, would be contacting our office to apprise us of happenings in their locale. Some were baffled by situations, some seeking counsel, others looking for affirmation for their way of meeting their particular problems.

One such I recall: a pastor from Iowa called and wanted to tell his story.

A White woman had moved to his little town and she wanted to transfer into this pastor's congregation. Complication: she had recently married a young Black

Lutheran. She wondered, would this young man be welcomed into this congregation?

"No problem!" The pastor continued, "Chairs could be placed in the little room next to the altar; the newcomers could sit there, hearing the readings and the sermon, and singing the hymns along with the worshippers in the pews. At that point in the liturgy when members would be kneeling at the altar to receive wafer and wine in celebrating the Lord's Supper, the Pastor would step into the little room and serve these two new members."

The pastor was obviously pleased with his solution to the couple's request. He had not even begun to realize that he was not solving a pastoral problem. Rather, he was communicating to his congregation that the young couple's worship life was not as important as the rest of the congregation's. In addition, he was denying the congregation the opportunity to be a welcoming home for this young couple.

There were the dozens of cases where pastors advised some Black would-be-members not to attend, lest some prejudiced white members or prospective members stay away or even leave the congregation.

Many did recognize the need for LHRAA's counsel and so LHRAA was called on to speak, submit articles, and participate in planning sessions to avert explosive responses to instances of severe tension. We were invited to address larger church body conventions on seven occasions. One of these was scheduled for a gathering of clergy persons in the South. Some of the invitees would be African-American so the organizers made arrangements for the convening to take place at a military base where racial identity would not be a factor.

On my trip to the military base in Florida, I was joined by Bob and Caroline Miller from Charlotte, North

Pastors Karl Lutze, Joe Ellwanger, and Will Herzfeld.

Carolina, Joe Ellwanger from Birmingham, Alabama, and Will Herzfeld, a Black pastor from Tuscaloosa, Alabama. The US military base at Pensacola could handle a desegregated program.

However, since the military personnel had already signed up for most of the beds, the pastoral conference would have to make its own arrangements for sleeping accommodations for delegates at local hotels. Caroline and Bob Miller had already been checked in.

Pastors Joe Ellwanger, Will Herzfeld, and I found our way to the hotel that had arranged reservations for others who would be in attendance at the conference. When we approached the registration counter, the desk clerk looked at the three of us and curtly addressed Joe and me, "For you two I have room." Then looking at Will, he said to him, "For you, I don't."

By this time, other people in the lobby had stopped their conversations to watch what was happening. Surely in his life, Will had encountered this kind of situation before. He turned, looked at me and said, "Come on, BOY, bring my bags. We're leaving here." I lifted the bags and we left. The cluster of people in the lobby who had stopped their own conversations to eavesdrop on our little drama seemed amazed—or amused—or, at the very least, baffled. They were used to a White man calling a Black man BOY, but never the reverse.

We climbed into our rental car, and made our way to a Black neighborhood. We stopped at a small gas station and asked where we might find a motel. The attendant gave us the directions to a modest cluster of cabins where we registered for the night. The particular door assigned to us opened to an unimpressive but adequate set of typical accommodations: dresser, lavatory, closet, table, and three folding chairs, a twin bed and one double bed. Quite unwilling and altogether unready to bow to any more of the South's segregation culture, I said, "Joe, you take the single bed and Will and I will share the double bed." We said our prayers and slept soundly, not even daring to wonder whether a local Klan group would approve.

The experience reminded me of an earlier day when I still lived in Oklahoma. That was in 1957. Representatives of different Urban League chapters in Southern metropolitan centers had been invited to attend a special conference in Atlanta. Marion Taylor, Director of our Tulsa Urban League, was driving and urged me to accompany him. We had eaten before leaving and at mid-afternoon when we stopped for fuel, he left me briefly. He had gone to the rear door of a small fast-serve cafe and returned with sandwiches and beverages for us to eat in the car as we resumed our trip. When we arrived in Memphis, he told me he had called ahead to a friend of his who headed the Black community's YMCA there and had already reserved overnight facilities for us.

The night was refreshing and in the morning, we made our way to a restaurant nearby. We entered and found a seat in a vacant booth. All the serving staff was African-American. So were all the customers. The atmosphere was congenial. Marion and I talked about the remaining miles of our journey. Twenty minutes had elapsed when we took notice that we had not been approached by any of the servers to place our order. My friend went to the cashier and returned, whispering a message of explanation, "They don't cater to White folks here!"

I quickly and naively replied, "O, tell them we don't need anything special. Just a small breakfast will be fine."

My friend Marion hastily explained: "There's a White policeman out in front ready to make arrests if this place is found serving Whites!"

In spite of the efforts to overturn laws and customs of White racism, there was much yet to be done. I remembered this again when I heard longtime Southern Black people say, "Everything has changed but nothing is different, and everything is different, but nothing has changed."

THE LUTHERAN CHURCH - MISSOURI SYNOD
210 NORTH BROADWAY • SAINT LOUIS 2, MISSOURI

CENTRAL 1-0869
AREA CODE 314

OFFICE OF THE
PRESIDENT

February 26, 1963

Lutheran Human Relations
Association of America
Valparaiso University
Valparaiso, Indiana

Greetings!

The Lutheran Human Relations Association of America has worked for ten years in the area of seeking recognition and help for minority groups in our beloved nation. This country, under God, from its beginnings has stood out in the world promising a haven of refuge and a land of opportunity.

This promise has not always developed all the fruit hoped for. The Lutheran Human Relations Association, however, has sought to remedy inequities though it has been difficult at times to do so. Indeed some have said that the organization "goes too far"; others have said that it "does too little."

Be assured that my office, in recognition of the sincere and conscientious concerns for good by a voluntary organization of fellow Christians and fellow members of The Lutheran Church - Missouri Synod, wishes you well on your Tenth Anniversary.

It is my personal prayer that my gracious Savior, without whom none of us is worth anything at all, would give you wisdom and understanding, wise counsel and patience and continued great care for holy Scripture.

May God in his bountiful kindness reward you for your service.

In Jesus' name

O. Harms

CHAPTER 9
LHRAA
AND LUTHERAN CHURCH BODIES

While neither his predecessor nor his successor as President of the Lutheran Church-Missouri Synod ever made public commendation of LHRAA's ministry, Oliver Harms did, on the occasion of LHRAA's Tenth Anniversary, send a message to all LCMS pastors on his official presidential letterhead to be printed on the cover of our *VANGUARD*, affirming and urging support for the leadership and service we were providing. This letter appeared on the front page of our publication, *The VANGUARD*.

In a personal note to me later, Dr. Harms told how many harsh letters he had received especially from pastors in the South, criticizing what he had done. Indicating how much such correspondence pained him, he pleaded, "Karl, I want to be supportive, but, please, don't rock the boat!" How could I not rock the boat? My own personal response was silence.

Increasingly, pastors—Black as well as White—who had been serving in African-American or racially changing communities were beginning to express their resentment at being regarded as "second-class citizens." Dr. Harms clearly was troubled by such comments and asked for my thoughts as to how he might best respond. He was eager to avoid being regarded as condescending.

I suggested that he invite all such pastors—Black and White—to a meeting in which they might be given opportunity to speak their hearts, to spill out their deeper feelings, to put into words what they felt the church body might do to enhance, support, and affirm these workers in their ministerings. In many ways during his role of leadership, President Harms demonstrated his skills in exercising the process of reconciliation that called for listening to troubled voices and seeking understanding, compromising, negotiating, collaborating, and engaging in mutual planning to effect constructive change.

He liked the idea and promptly proceeded with plans for arranging the event. At least 90 church workers, Black and White—most of them clergy—came to the meeting. Some at first seemed hesitant in voicing their hurts, fearing that criticizing of the church administrators might jeopardize whatever favorable relations may have already existed or that financial subsidy for their work might be reduced, should they appear unappreciative. As participants began to speak up to air their grievances, the criticisms mounted and the complaints increased—and the event seemed to be crumbling to the point of being a grumbling session. The invitees to the session time and again spoke words that indicated the experience of being regarded as "second-class" citizens in the Lutheran community. Their faces and voices clearly displayed disappointment; disillusionment and frustration were seen on faces and heard in voices.

It was a difficult moment for Dr. Harms. To maintain an attitude of respect for these church workers as they emotionally voiced critical comments, he would turn the presiding of the meeting to Dr. Wiederaenders, his vice-president, who continued to invite members of the audience to make their comments. Communications seemed to fall farther apart.

Finally, it was the White Reverend Richard John Neuhaus, first President of our New York Chapter of LHRAA and longtime pastor in New York's inner city, and master of eloquence, who rose and put the issues in perspective. He simply said that so many, many White people—church leaders, pastors and laity, too—have not had the kind of experience that the people gathered in this room had probably had. Then he told his story:

> *The scene was a crowded public health clinic. An African-American mother was sitting there, sobbing. She had been holding her hoarse-voiced, coughing infant for more than three hours. Now, still waiting in line, she watched the little one in her arms die. And the pastor was called on to comfort her.*

"All the pastors gathered here in this room," Neuhaus explained, "have stories of their own to tell. They are speaking out in their deep desire today to enlist church leaders and White pastors and their White congregations to be true allies, who will supportively stand with them as they seek to address the needs of disadvantaged, unwelcomed and largely resented newly arrived neighbors and their children. These workers here who confront the problems of the troubled, day after day, in the spirit of St. Paul ask '. . . and we burn not?'

"Their appeal today is 'Do not walk by on the other side!'"

In this situation, there was no favorable response from President Harms or Vice President Wiederaenders, who was at his side. There was no indication that they really had grasped what these pastors and teachers were saying—or that they as leaders of the church they represented were committed to contribute to this dialog, offering a positive response to resolve the debilitating situation in which they were involved and which was being described to them so powerfully.

* * * * *

In the early 1960s, the number of people who in some way were in communication with LHRAA probably numbered nearly 4,000. This consisted of those who came to our Institutes at Valpo, plus those who joined our chapters, as well as those who supported us with contributions and all others who received our bimonthly newsletter, *The VANGUARD*, which detailed current happenings on the race relations scene.

Since Andrew Schulze and I were both ordained clergy of the LCMS, and since most of the estimated 132,000 African-American Lutherans in the USA were served and supported by the ministry of the LCMS, it was logical that the most immediate arena for our addressing segregating patterns and practices afflicting Lutherans was my own LCMS and, of course, its leaders and congregations.

Among other Lutherans, the structures of the church bodies found their practices and policies less than helpful in staving off the hesitancy and effectiveness of speaking up and standing tall in the face of patterns of exclusion and superiority towards people of color. For the most part, the leaders among non-Missouri Synod Lutherans showed a tremendous respect for the spirit and programs of LHRAA. Their experience with what we were doing and growing communication with us won their good will, appreciation and friendship. We were asked to speak at their conventions. And their leaders' were frequently in attendance at our programs and Institutes.

In another meeting with LCMS's President, Oliver Harms, who continued to be a warm, yet somewhat cautious supporter of LHRAA, I mentioned that more and more representatives of the American Lutheran Church (ALC) and Lutheran Church in American (LCA) had been attending our Institutes at Valparaiso. I remember him saying, "Karl, there's no need for beginning two more organizations like LHRAA to serve each of those church bodies. Since LHRAA is an independent organization, why don't you invite people of those two bodies to join with you?"

And we did. Both Dr. Robert Marshall who headed LCA and Dr. Frederick Schiotz, President of the ALC, accepted our invitation and participated as speakers in our annual Institutes in Valparaiso.

The doors of the Presidents of the three major Lutheran church bodies were always open to my visits. I remember one occasion when, at short notice, I was scheduled to be at meetings in Minneapolis for two days. I recalled a phone conversation I'd had with President Schiotz a few weeks earlier, in which he had invited me to come to his office when I next would be in the Twin Cities.

Dr. Robert Marshall.

Before finalizing any other appointments for my time there, I called Dr. Schiotz. I was sure that he might well have a less flexible calendar during my time there. I should have known—he was already committed for different time slots I'd reserved for meetings in my Minnesota stopover. But, to my surprise, he suggested an early morning breakfast session from 6 'til 7:45 A.M. at a restaurant close to the hotel where I would be staying.

Requests made to LHRAA for specific information or services often came from the ALC which at the time sponsored eleven congregations in the United States, designated as "Negro Missions." Most African-Americans served by the Lutheran Church in America were located in small parishes in the Caribbean islands. A sprinkling of African-American members in northern urban centers was also served by LCA congregations there.

Dr. Frederick Schiotz.

John Houck and Herluf Jensen, at that time both staff executives on the two other church bodies, identified for us people in their respective organizations who would serve well if added to LHRAA's Board. Subsequently, Board members were elected for three-year terms. Thereafter at annual election meetings ballots provided LHRAA members gave them a choice to vote for one of two persons nominated from each of the three national Lutheran Churches. This, of course, meant that each of the three church bodies would be equally represented on the Board at its meetings.

I had never met Herluf Jensen but we had talked together on the phone and corresponded. I learned that while attending Harvard, he had been a leader in a Christian student association and in that role became a friend of Bill Ellis, who was a year or so behind him in that program. They became close friends. Ellis even filled the role of sponsor at a Jensen child's baptism. Herluf thought so highly of Ellis that he nominated him as a candidate for election to LHRAA's Board. Bill Ellis was elected and after serving only a short time, he was elected LHRAA's president, succeeding the Reverend Clemonce Sabourin, Pastor of Mount Zion Lutheran Church in Harlem, New York.

Through the years, I have been blessed to meet some superb Christian church leaders, but I have never met one as genuinely humble or more totally pastoral than Bishop Herluf Jensen.

We were sipping coffee together when he blushingly told me the story of the hours that involved his being named to the post of Bishop. It all happened when, during a convention, his predecessor announced to the delegates present his intention to resign from his position effective at the close of the meeting. He explained the procedure of nominating and subsequent election that would ulti-mately name the person who would succeed him.

As the program continued, four names were pro-posed for the ballot.

As I recall, the two persons who received the most votes had each received almost 100 votes. Unexpectedly, both rose to ask that their names be withdrawn from the slate. Herluf's name had received only one vote. He said "Can you imagine how presumptuous and ludicrous it would have been for me, with only one vote, to have raised my hand to say, 'I also wish to remove my name from the ballot?'

"The presiding Bishop then announced that since the other remaining candidate and I had garnered only a few votes, he wanted to be sure all of the voting delegates would have opportunity to know as much about us as possible. He would postpone the vote until the next morning. He asked that each of us prepare a few paragraphs telling a bit about our experiences and also how we would envision our serving were we to be elected.

"I didn't know the other gentleman at all. He was called on to speak first. I felt he really had made a good presentation. When it was my turn I stepped to the microphone and told how much I appreciated the words of the alternative candidate we had all just heard and that I would feel very good about his being my bishop.

"Then I told the assembly that, paraphrasing Woody Allen (a film comedian of his time), I didn't know if I would want to belong to a church body that had me as its Bishop!"

Herluf then said, "The audience roared with laughter and voted me their Bishop."

CHAPTER 10

DENVER—LCMS CONVENTION AND MUTUAL ENRICHMENT GRANT

O liver Harms was a warm, gentle person who strongly desired to fill a pastoral role in the conduct of his presidency. Before taking office he had served as pastor of a large congregation in Houston, Texas. He truly had understood the feelings of his parishioners and was sensitive to their uneasiness about race. They

Dr. Oliver Harms

were fearful of the increased efforts that the government was investing in the elimination of racial segregation which had marked the way of life of so many people in their church, in their country and in its institutions.

Dr. Harms did not seem to realize that by condoning the church members' insistence on segregation he was affirming their subordinating of Black brothers and sisters, denying them status and full membership and acceptance in the family of Jesus Christ.

Dr. Harms wanted to be helpful but in his efforts to "not rock the boat," he did not see that his actions affirmed the very issues LHRAA was addressing. His lack of understanding was further displayed in another visit I had with him in 1965.

It was the Monday after "Bloody Sunday" (March 7, 1965), which had muddied the name of Selma, Alabama. Of course, we had all seen the news clips of the previous afternoon that showed law enforcement officers on horseback with clubs and pipes and the tear gas attacks on hundreds of churchly, justice-seeking demonstrators on the Edmund Pettus Bridge. So that was the launching pad of the conversation that ensued.

As we spoke, I was amazed at his assessment of the incident. He said, "Yes, I saw the film last evening. But you know, Karl, they can do amazing things with the camera and other electronic tools to make things look more dramatic than they really were."

I responded, "Dr. Harms, to reproduce that film would have called for manufacturing hundreds of frames and restructuring them—a process that would probably take hours of technically skilled workers trying to depict people being struck and wounded. This was filmed when it occurred and the film had captured exactly what happened. This is not a time to find excuses for what happened nor to quote Luther's counsel and to put the best construction on everything. This was exposure of evil and the church must speak out on behalf of its victims." And that prompted a preparation of steps Dr. Harms and I might take to identify himself—and our church—on the side of justice and non-violence.

I continued to meet with Dr. Harms and every time I would come to St. Louis, he would welcome me into his office and close the door behind him, with instructions that we were not to be interrupted. Then, instead of staying behind his huge desk, he would come around to a chair that faced mine, with a pad and pen in his hand. And the conversation would usually be launched by his words, "All right, Karl, tell me what I should be knowing now about what is current in civil rights and what I might do as a faithful leader of the church."

On one such occasion, in 1966, I suggested that he might appoint a special committee, a "President's Advisory Council," to keep him apprised of interracial issues that impinged upon the Christian community. He was pleased with the suggestion and asked whom I might nominate for such a role.

The names would quickly be recognized by people involved in race relations: Pastor William Griffen, pastor of Christ the King Church in Chicago's farther south side; Dr. Jeff Johnson, Social Work Professor at Valparaiso University; Ms. Georgia Falwell, East St. Louis Integrated School faculty and member of Board of Directors or LHRAA; Pastor Arthur Simon, founder of Bread for the World; Pastor Erwin Kurth, inner-city ministries, Detroit, Brooklyn and Los Angeles; Dr. Norman Kretzmann, Pastor and religious journalist, Minneapolis; Chris McNair, father of Denise, victim of Birmingham's 16th Street Church bombing, high school vocational counselor; Dr. Dean Lueking, author, Pastor of Grace Church in

Caroline Miller   Dean Lueking

Chris McNair   Norman Kretzmann

Georgia Falwell   Erwin Kurth

William Griffen   Jeff Johnson

Arthur Simon   Karl Lutze

River Forest, IL; Ms. Caroline Miller, LHRAA Board Member from Charlotte, NC and myself.

He was pleased with the suggestions and invited each to serve. All accepted. Not much later we came together for our first meeting. The exchanging of ideas was stimulating and the spirit hopeful.

Perhaps it was at coffee break that one of our group mentioned that when he had served on other committees, the nearby Missouri Athletic Club had invited the Lutherans to utilize their facilities for their special meetings. Dr. Harms listed some of the benefits derived in accepting the Club's generous hospitality through the years. It was very convenient, very comfortable, very plush, and very exclusive.

Then Dr. Harms attempted to explain that the meetings of our Council would not be held there. It at once became clear:

the African-Americans in our group would not be welcome at the Club.

Each in our group could hardly believe what we were hearing. Dr. Harms told us that the Club had been offering this hospitality for several years whenever some Synodical group was meeting in St. Louis; he didn't want to offend the Club leadership by insisting that African-Americans be served there.

The head of our church was in effect saying, "We don't want to hurt the feelings of these people who have been so gracious and generously kind to us through the years, and we surely think our African-American brothers and sisters would understand."

The committee unanimously indicated that Synod was failing to take a stand against any idea that might imply that some of their members had racial privilege. The Synod should have no part in such exclusiveness. We tendered our resignation from the council and heard no further word on the matter from the President's office.

Dr. Harms continued in his office through these turbulent years in our country and then came the 1969 Convention of the Lutheran Church-Missouri Synod.

In many denominations, church bodies have national conventions every two to three years to allow congregations and their leaders the opportunity to review the performance of their church bodies and to chart a direction for the days that lie ahead.

The pattern for these meetings provides for laity as well as pastors to be equally representing their congregations "back home" (from all over the country). At these gatherings, they consider the reports of elected national leaders and their staff assistants as well recommendations for the years ahead.

As ideally fair and democratic the intended concept, many of the less informed elected delegates to the conventions often turn to some more experienced delegates sitting near to ask how they should vote on various issues.

Beside the agenda prepared for the 1969 LCMS national convention itself, people brought a great many other agendas with them to Denver: race relations, concern about synodical leadership, fellowship with other church bodies, status of women in the church and, increasingly challenging governmental decisions, the issue of prolonging military conflict with Vietnam, changing social patterns, cooperation with government, worship, public and faith issues, and more.

Never before had an organized bloc of delegates been enlisted to challenge the leadership of the Synod's incumbent President and to engage in political action to replace him. When votes were counted, President of Concordia Seminary in Springfield, IL, Dr. J. A. O. Preus, was named successor to Dr. Oliver Harms, effective upon the close of the convention. Dr. Harms continued to preside for the remaining days of this convention and did so with impressive grace—so much so that some who had been persuaded to vote him out of office expressed regret for having voted against him.

In the months preceding the convention, Dr. Harms had been helpful in readying his church for fellowship with the ALC. But even prior to the convention his newly elected successor, Jacob Preus, had announced his own opposition to "declaration of fellowship" with the ALC, of which his own cousin, David, was President. Though Jake won the election to the presidency, the delegates nonetheless passed the resolution establishing ties between LCMS and ALC.

Recognizing these as days of racial unrest in our country, President Harms, in preparing the assembly agenda, had allocated time on the program for a message to the convention from LHRAA's President, Atty. William Ellis, of New York, himself a member of the LCA Board of Trustees. Meanwhile, largely by the planning of Pastors Will Herzfeld and Albert Pero, all African-American clergy present were asked to step forward and mount the platform so that the delegates might be introduced to these workers and that their ministerings, little noticed or appreciated in the church, might be acknowledged and affirmed in this very public gathering.

A motion from the floor asked that the convention commit the church to stand with these ministries, especially in view of the tension and disruptive turbulence that marked the time. The motion invited conventioneers to follow these workers out of the convention room at this moment to join them in prayerful contemplation, before returning to the hall thirty minutes later so that the work of the convention might resume.

President Harms, slightly befuddled, desiring to respect the Black members of the church, yet eager to attend to the items on the busy agenda, attempted to resist the proposed disruptions. But the Black clergy left the stage; delegates left their seats and in quiet dignity simply followed them out of the convention room. The President had no choice but to speak into the microphone and announce that the session would resume in one half hour.

And the convention did resume again after this interruption of the program in tribute to the African-American leaders.

This was a dramatic moment in the history of Missouri Synod and its impact on the lives of literally thousands of Black church workers and laity.

Prior to the convention we at LHRAA had developed a program called "Mutual Enrichment" which would involve professors of theology from Lutheran seminaries and universities becoming involved with clergy in inner city churches.

We were much concerned that pastors in inner-city situations be available for doing their post-graduate studies during summer months—the very time the riots were threatening to burst in the places where their ministry is most needed.

In response and with the help of grants from Wheat Ridge Ministries and other foundations, we launched the program called "Mutual Enrichment." The "mutual" aspect anticipated these grants that would serve both inner-city pastors and theology professors.

The grant would provide a modest stipend and expenses for a pastor and a theologian to spend two weeks together at the site of such an inner-city congregation. Every weekday morning, the theologian would be lecturing on a theological topic which student and scholar both concurred as desirable. Once noon had passed, the pastor became the teacher with the professor following everywhere the pastor led (that might include hospitals, neighborhood meetings, visits to federal housing apartments and the like.)

One provision was that the visiting theologian was not to preach the next Sunday nor to do any other programs for the congregation. He was to be student and the host pastor, his teacher. He was to be in the congregation and later comment on the pastor's sermon. At the end of the two weeks, they would evaluate each other's performance and suggest adjustments in style, patterns of ministry and effectiveness.

One of the participants in the program was a campus colleague who was also Dean of Valparaiso's Chapel, Dr. Norman Nagel. The report of his experience, appearing in *The VANGUARD* upon his return, tells the story of what the program meant to participants.

Mutual Enrichment Program

Ghetto Life: Loving – Caring
by Norman E. Nagel

This summer in Holden Village I saw the figure of a black Christ standing where everybody gathers together in the evening around a fire. In the Cascade Mountains summer is cool.

Last summer Pastor Herzfeld was there and spoke of the black Christ. Some were shocked. One man bitterly opposed the idea. There was heated talk, and out of it all came a widening understanding and deeper sense of responsibility. A black brother had put it hard and straight, and struck home in some white hearts.

They were not pushed apart by it, but were finally pulled closer together, for they were drawn together by Christ.

Last summer I was a white pastor assigned to a black congregation in Detroit in the Mutual Enrichment Program of LHRAA. Almost every evening I was a guest in another home. They had such a pastor that made them feel a pastor is a man you can trust, so there was not so much walking round each other but more dealing straight. Many an evening Christ came through black and clear.

In the afternoons pastors from roundabout came to Nazareth and we studied theology together: our worship of Christ, the liturgy that runs from Sunday though all the days of the week. The neighbor Roman Catholic priest was also with us. In the ghetto Christians pull together better, it seems, than most places.

In the mornings I got a glimpse of different kinds of life in Detroit: individual missions, hospitals, Ford plant, courts and prisons, social agencies, adoption centers and political committees. You see things when you sit a few hours in a big city hospital waiting room, or attend the preliminary hearing of a man charged with murdering a policeman. People live so near to violence and yet so desperately little is done to remove what breeds it.

Yet people care for people in ways that one does not so much find in the suburbs. In the home in which I lived, people and especially children suddenly appeared and were made to be welcome and at home. Somebody had to go to the hospital and so the kids piled in to stay as long as necessary. Christ shone through – black.

For me it was a size of enrichment that I could not have imagined. Something had to die in me to make room for all that enrichment. How much enrichment there was for anybody else, I don't know. Blessings work both ways, I could not have been given so much without there being blessing also for those who gave.

When I had met earlier with Dr. Preus—then President of Concordia Seminary in Springfield, IL, I asked him whether he might suggest a member of his faculty as one who might benefit from participating in the program; his response was, "I probably would benefit from that myself, so sign me up."

At the Denver Convention, I bumped into Dr. Preus again. At the end of a session as we were stepping onto a crowded elevator, I was near the front of the car and raised my voice to be heard by him standing in the far rear. I said to him, "I imagine you will not want to participate in our Mutual Enrichment Program, now that you will be starting your new job."

And he, with clear voice, responded, "That's a good program. I probably need it more than I had thought when I first applied." And, indeed, he and Mrs. Preus both participated in a condensed one-week program which we arranged for them in Chicago.

I, personally, found much to criticize in the way President Preus exercised his new position. I thought that in many respects he contributed to a significant divisiveness that ultimately caused a break-away by some of the brightest and strongest members of LCMS. As did many others, I missed the efforts to effect unity in the church as it became clearer and clearer that he had given strong leadership to a bloc of voting members at the next convention of the Synod who effectively achieved the Synod's withdrawal from fellowship with the American Lutheran Church, the tie that had been established at the Denver Convention.

I could not admire such leadership. But he was such an enigma. I must tell you of a time I was in a remote area of the Los Angeles airport. As I passed by I saw him sitting quite alone, not another person anywhere near and he was reading from a small book. He had not noticed me. I walked past him again, wondering if my eyes had deceived me. It was he—and I recognized the book. It was a copy of the New Testament in the original Greek language. He was not reading it for show. Here was a scholar having a private devotion, wanting to be nurtured by the Word of God.

CHAPTER 11
DISCOVERED LINKAGES—
DIFFERENT AGENDAS

O n one occasion, I accepted an invitation to meet with national leaders of the other Lutheran church bodies, which revealed the strengthening of ties with other leaders whose roots were not in LCMS. I was pleased to be a guest.

Attorney Ellis was a member of the LCA and of its Board of Directors. President of the LCA at the time was the Reverend Dr. Franklin Clark Fry, a highly respected and venerable church-man. I was particularly pleased at this recognition of LHRAA's ministry.

Attorney William Ellis.

I do not know whether the LCA was taking a leaf from Missouri's agenda, but in his position on his church's social ministry staff at the time, Herluf Jensen had set up a meeting in New York in which the Black clergymen would sit in session with Dr. Fry to express their com-plaints about their functioning within the LCA structure. Since Ellis was the only non-White member of the Church's Board at the time, he was invited to be present. And Herluf invited me as well.

By way of beginning the meeting, the owner of an African-American bookstore in New York's Harlem addressed the gathering. His remarks were clearly militant, and cogent, as he asked the clergy audience to recognize their responsibility in thinking through their role in the days ahead.

The African-Americans present had the floor and, with increasing fervor, criticized the church structure for its lethargic response to interracial problems. President Fry had sat quietly through the discussions. At last, he rose to give a response.

It was clear that he had been offended by the comments. Then, citing the many ways in which the Church body had made special concessions and provided financial support to Black congregations and their pastors, without explicitly spelling out the words, he implied that he regarded these voices as ungrateful and manifested his own personal hurt from the things these men had said. Attorney Ellis was obviously disappointed in Dr. Fry's comments, the man for whom he had such profound respect.

I don't recall how the meeting came to its quick, abrupt, and awkward end. I was embarrassed to be present and wished that I might have been able to hide under the nearest chair and leave. I vividly remember seeing Bill Ellis obviously experiencing great emotional pain, storming right past me through the open door to the street, eager to escape the scene.

I hurried to the elevator to return to my hotel room. When the elevator doors opened, Dr. Fry was there, about to enter the car. Upon seeing me, he stepped back into the waiting space he'd been leaving and, greeting me, he motioned me to sit with him. The formalities were brief: he was glad to see me and pleased that I had come to visit. Then—altogether unexpectedly—he said, "I noted your presence as I responded to the critical remarks our Black brothers had spoken; it seemed to me you were disappointed in my words to them."

I was dumbfounded at his remark and quite unready to comment, however, I remember saying, "Dr. Fry, from where I was seated, I was able to watch these men as they would stand up to make their statements. What I had seen were men, standing tall. Their voices became clearer and stronger as they spoke, their shoulders thrown back, their heads held high, showing an air of confidence, saying what they felt compelled to say as they had never done before. I thought to myself what a wonderful display of recognition to have invited these men to participate in this kind of conversation.

"And then you spoke—words that were true, reminding them how your church has wanted to be supportive of these disciples. However, when they heard your words, they felt reprimanded. They found themselves regarded as ungrateful children in the family. I could see them— visibly—slumping in their seats, quieted, shamed." He spoke gracious words of thanks and we parted.

There was little need for more words. When I arrived home days later, I found an envelope awaiting me in the mail. It contained no note—just a very generous personal check for our LHRAA ministry, signed by Franklin Clark Fry.

There were other LCA events that related to the work on civil rights. Each of these events had a significant effect on my energy and insights in the years to come.

I recall one occasion that was particularly memorable to me.

I had just spent two particularly intensive days conducting a workshop in the Twin Cities before boarding a late night train to Chicago where I was to address a conference of LCA clergy gathered to discuss the challenge presented to our Lord's people in this time of interracial tensions.

I felt my presentation had gone well, but I felt totally exhausted, never so totally wiped out. Two more speakers were to follow me and in an afternoon session, the three of us were to respond to questions from the audience. I had taken a seat on a rear pew as the program continued but I had become totally restless. I couldn't begin to focus on what the people up front were saying.

The host pastor's young assistant noticed my discomfort and led me to his little apartment in the church tower. I took to his couch. He left me. Couldn't sleep. Couldn't concentrate. Sipped some coffee and woke to the realization I didn't know where I was. I slipped down the steps and found the out-of-doors. The fresh air was good and I decided to walk. I walked and I walked. I bought a magazine. And an apple. Ate it. I spotted a park bench, sat down, and I read a few pages of my magazine.

I knew I had to get back to the church and I hoped I could find it. I walked and walked and suddenly there it was. The Lutheran Church. I still have no remembrance of its name. As I entered, everything seemed quite empty; no one in sight. But there, inside the entrance, was a casket, its occupant apparently awaiting "a visitation hour." Bizarre!

By now, I began to hear the muffled sound of ministers who had gone down to the church's undercroft for lunch and for the afternoon's closing sessions. And I joined them. The host pastor apparently had not noted my absence. He had been able to stay and handed me a small sheet of paper with a message for me, from Robert Marshall, whom I later had the privilege of knowing in his role as successor to Dr. Franklin Clark Fry, LCA's president.

His message: he regretted deeply having to leave early because he really appreciated my presentation and wished he might have heard more of my words in the afternoon.

That afternoon presentation went well and I was eager to get home and be with my family.

P.S. Never again have I experienced a recurrence of my scary episode of exhaustion.

CHAPTER 12:

UNPREDICTABLE CONNECTIONS

Don Larsen: I met Don Larsen during our days as students at Concordia Seminary in St. Louis. We sang together in three different choirs during our time there. More than a dozen years later, we had many more occasions to see and work with each other. During the in-between years while I served parishes in Black communities in Oklahoma, Don was pastor in racially changing communities in Detroit. He now was a staff person for the National Lutheran Council (which later became the Lutheran Council, USA), an inter-Lutheran agency that served to coordinate ministries of the major Lutheran church bodies. Meanwhile, I had begun my work with LHRAA. Don attended LHRAA Board meetings, but these occasions hardly provided us with much time for relaxed visiting and conversation before going our separate ways.

Rev. Donald Larson
Photo by Stebbins

We were in New York on August 16th, 1965, a very warm day. As our meeting ended, Don and I compared our return-to-Chicago flight schedules. To our surprise, we had both been booked to fly out of LaGuardia for Chicago on United Airlines flight 389. We checked with United reservations and were able to reserve seats on a later flight, allowing us time for dinner together and a longer visit as well. Once we had boarded and were settled in our seats, we commented on how gratifying it was that we had been able to work out our change of plans.

It was not until the next morning that we learned the fate of the flight we had cancelled. When nearing Chicago, it had plunged into Lake Michigan and all thirty aboard had been killed. I don't remember any subsequent visit when Don and I would be together again that we didn't recall the astonishing climax of that day.

In the months that followed, I kept on flying. My tightly-packed calendar scheduled me to attend meetings and appointments in every geographic direction. By this time, we had more than fifty chapters of LHRAA. My responsibilities at the University had also increased. I would often find myself "on the road" three or more days of a week. A phone call from my good friend Elmer Witt (who was now Executive Director of the Walther League) asked me to take on an additional assignment. He knew full well how demanding my schedule had been, but he was hoping that what he was asking would provide a change of pace, a chance to catch my breath a bit. He asked me to spend a week at a camp with youth near Red Lodge, Montana.

Two adult counselors would be on hand to assist me in a five-day stay, leading some thirty people of high school age in a program of Bible Study, recreation, singing, creative writing, and worship. I agreed to help out.

Good program, good setting, good staff, good kids—altogether a good week. Well, pretty good. One young fellow just didn't seem to fit. I don't recall his name—I'll call him Larry.

When it came time to choose a lead player for various contests and games, he'd always step forward to the head of the line. When groups of campers with similar interests would be sitting together at meal time, Larry would invariably choose a place in the middle of one. When questions were posed for discussion time, he'd be first to raise his hand or to answer before being called on. Staff members found him pushy and overbearing; we agreed his presence was often obtrusive. The campers themselves were more obvious in their resentment of his self-assertiveness.

For the Thursday evening session, by way of assessing the week's experience, the campers had been given the assignment to write an essay telling about themselves and what the highlight of their stay had been. They were to read their piece to the group.

I called on them in alphabetical order, and as it happened, Larry's turn came last. He stood. With a softer voice than he normally had used, he started reading. He told us his dad was a farmer and they lived on a large ranch. There were no people his age living within miles. Larry had no brothers or sisters. His dad was his very best friend. His dad was very much involved in some national agricultural organization. Larry's mother and he would drive him to the airport and call for him again upon his return.

As Larry continued reading his essay, we learned how almost a year had passed since his dad again had been away for such a meeting. As usual, Larry and his mom had made the trip to the airport to meet him. When they arrived, they were told that the flight would be late. They waited and waited. The plane's arrival was delayed even longer. They were told to return home and they would be called and informed as to when the arrival time would be announced. After long hours of waiting, there had been no call.

The next morning, the sheriff's car came up their long driveway. He told them the bitter news that Larry's dad's plane, on that leg of its trip between New York and Chicago, had plunged into Lake Michigan. Larry's father and all others aboard that flight had died.

Then Larry read the last paragraph of his essay, in which he told of the loneliness that was his since his dad, who'd been his very best friend, had died. And he added a word of gratitude to God for all the kindness and caring he had been experiencing with these new friends he had been with this week.

Everything was quiet as we gathered for our customary evening round of cookies and hot chocolate. But this time it was different. It seemed everyone wanted to sit near Larry—surely a bit ashamed, but grateful for the love he'd shown us.

And I remembered my colleague in ministry, Don Larsen, for Larry's father had died on Flight 389, the one we had not taken.

CHAPTER 13

MORE THAN BLACK AND WHITE— NATIVE AMERICAN

A s powerful as the voice of LHRAA was becoming for racial equality, LHRAA'S voice was becoming the voice for even more inclusiveness.

As author Kathryn Galchutt remarked in her book *The Career of Andrew Schulze*, Andrew had been, for some time, pressing for the passing of a resolution at the LCMS convention encouraging ministry among "neglected groups" such as "Asian, Jewish, Hispanic, and Native Americans, as well as anonymous 'lost' men and women in the slums and on the skid rows of our cities."

Invited to address a group of church workers assembled for exploring ways of involving Lutherans with Native Americans, he was deeply impressed with suggestions for greater co-operative efforts by all Lutheran church bodies. So when I arrived at LHRAA, Andrew said "Karl, if I were to attend the next meeting, I would be spreading myself too thin. So I am asking you to attend the next meeting of this group at Estes Park in Colorado."

The experience was new to me, but I was eager to do anything that Andrew deemed helpful. I can't remember the precise number of people present but only one of the possibly 30 or so was Native American.

The discussion topics revolved around dealing with alcoholism, improving reservation sanitation concerns, and making materials available for children's study of Bible stories. Trying to make a contribution to the discussion, I pointed out that though I knew little about the Native American scene, the U.S. government's Bureau of Indian Affairs was probably working on the first two of these items. Our task, I suggested, should be capturing the attention of churches and enlisting their members' involvement in ministry, and this ought be considered as a primary concern. They concurred and asked me to return next year and present a theological background for such ministry.

This was an early lesson for me to remember when participating with well-intentioned groups. A person making a suggestion for a fresh area of concern is very likely to be assigned the role of leader in the new committee to make plans for successful execution.

I accepted the role of essayist for the following year's meeting. My presentation was well received, as was the suggestion that this group might well become an organization, patterned somewhat like LHRAA. Its purpose: to involve churches in developing a structure that would collaborate with Native Americans in planning a useful and effective relationship.

Again there were no negative criticisms of the idea but an expanded questioning of how this relationship might look. I proposed formal invitations to Native Americans to participate in the project, drawing on their experience and wisdom. The group was enthusiastically responsive to this. Recognizing that many Native Americans who might be invited to help us might well not be Lutherans, the project could be called "Lutheran Church and Indian People," a title that was abbreviated to the letters LuCHIP.

Not only was there enthusiastic response to the idea but also the group appointed me to serve as the first President of LuCHIP. And of course this demonstrates the validity of my earlier lesson. If I hadn't suggested the idea, I would have been spared what resulted in a lot of new work for me. However, all this opened wide a door to my becoming a learner in a field in which I had only the most meager knowledge or experience.

Furthermore, all that occurred made possible my getting to know and work with some wonderful people whom I otherwise would probably never have met, several of whom became some of my dearest friends. My working with them helped open the wider world into which I was entering.

CHAPTER 14

RESPECT FOR A NAME—
SCHLACHTENHAUFEN

I don't recall with any kind of precise accuracy what the occasion was, but once again I was serving on a committee, this one assigned to plan some sort of academic event to which off-campus guests would be invited. The group agreed that the program should draw together as large an audience as possible. One member of the group added, "Then we should really engage a big name as speaker for the occasion." In the moment of silence that ensued, I succumbed to a mischievous response, "I have just the name: Joel Schlachtenhaufen."

After the groans subsided, I explained my momentary departure from our task at hand. This was not a fictitious

Joel Schlachtenhaufen

name. There really is a Joel Schlachtenhaufen—a very dear friend of mine, a clergyman serving in the New York offices of the Lutheran Council, USA (LCUSA). Although his field was not in the area of the program we were to develop in this meeting, during the coffee break that followed, several of the committee members wanted to hear more about this "big-name friend" of mine.

I gladly obliged. Joel's position was to assist the three major church bodies (ALC, LCA and LCMS) to develop opportunities of sharing the conduct and support of ministry, to expand services without duplicating efforts and expenditures. My connections with him were the result of my position as one of the four executive committee members of the National Indian Lutheran Board (NILB).

When I first met Joel, he conceded that it was not at all unusual for people to register surprise when introduced to him and not only because his name was "big." People of German roots would readily know the name (in English) for Schlachtenhaufen would be "slaughter pile." Joel had played football when enrolled at Drake University. In good humor, cheerleaders would take to the field and invite the crowd to respond to their spelling out his name, "Give me an "S..." the fans would repeat "S..." and the spelling would continue through a few more letters until the moment came when they feigned forgetting the sequence and started in again with "Give me an S . . . !"

Occasionally when I'd drop him a letter, I would join in such mischief, and address the envelope in large longhand so that I'd provide only enough space for the first syllable of his name and the letters "tenhaufen" would appear on the reverse of the envelope.

As humorous as the uses of Joel's surname were, it did have a practical benefit, at least once. On this occasion, one of the tribal communities in the Dakotas was confronted with a special emergency need. They invited NILB to make an appeal to present the story of their need to a committee representing all three Lutheran church groups. NILB decided to bring an elder person from that western tribal community to New York to make the presentation and to give a personal response to any questions the three Lutheran leaders might raise.

This man's experience and life had largely been limited to the reservations. He had thoroughly been immersed in the Native American experience and had little or no familiarity with the land of the White man. And he certainly had never set his foot into the precincts of a place like New York City. The LCUSA staff appointed their colleague, Joel, to be his guide while he was their guest during his stay in the city. Tickets for his flight had been sent and, when he arrived in New York, Joel Schlachtenhaufen was on hand to bring him to the site appointed for the very important meeting.

His presentation was both eloquent and persuasive and proved most effective. NILB's executive, Gene Crawford, himself a Sioux Indian, and Joel Schlachten-haufen, attended the session. Since the hours had been tiring and lengthy, though very successful, they planned a special ending for the remarkable day, worthy of celebration.

The restaurant they chose for an elegant dinner was a notch above the kind you might find in their guest's little home town—a full orchestra, fancy and elegantly set tables, a specially clad serving staff, and candles. They were barely settled at their table when their server appeared, ready to take their beverage order. Awed by the elaborate menu and a bit overwhelmed, their Dakota guest asked that the waiter bring the same drink he had seen him deliver moments before to a neighboring table.

After his first sip, their guest found the tall glass delicious, refreshing, and deserving of a quick refill. Soon the guest asked for directions to the men's room. They pointed the way to him and then settled into ordering their dinner. And they waited for their friend. And they waited. And he didn't return. And they waited. And they began to worry. And they checked the men's room. And he wasn't there. And they asked the bartender. He answered, "You mean that Indian?"

Impatiently, the man explained that he had "walked past one of our musicians and they started arguing and then fighting and we don't allow that here and two of our men put him right out that door!"

Leaving their dinners behind, Gene and Joel fanned out on the block they were in and, after that, to two neighboring blocks. No one had seen a man of his description. By now, hours had passed. Frustrated and very tired, the two men had no ideas left for finding the man who had been their responsibility. They decided to return to the apartment where Joel lived.

When they arrived, they found their guest sitting on the step to Joel's doorway. They were immensely relieved and grateful, but totally at a loss as to even imagine where their missing friend had been since they were separated and how he had arrived at this place. And he told his story.

He explained that the police had found him wandering about. In frisking him, they had found his airline ticket in his pocket, so they had driven him out to LaGuardia to put him on the flight his ticket named. But since the airlines aren't about to board people who might be regarded as "under the influence," the airport personnel denied him boarding. Since he was still in custody, the police asked if he knew anyone in the city.

He answered "Yes: Joel Schlachtenhaufen." He surprised the police who asked him if he could spell that name. He could. And he did.

The police checked a phone directory and there it was—the only Schlachtenhaufen in the book and the address with it. "And so they dropped me off here."

Chapter 15:
Limited Funds,
Creative Colleagues, Big Surprises

Marlo and Ted and a Wider World

It was the summer of 1968 and at every level—national, district, local parish, pastoral study —the uneasiness and/or unwillingness of the church to deal responsibly with race relations issues was apparent. We had to conduct LHRAA's ministry with severely limited financial underpinnings. Of inestimable value to the launching of the Association were the long hours, the skills, the experience, and the commitment that Margaret Schulze, Esther Lutze—and all others in our office and from across the country—brought to the scene.

Through the years more such dedicated women found their way to our ranks as members of our staff family. One such was Marlo Tellschow. She was a Valpo alumna. After graduating with high honors, rather than pursue other professional career tracks, she joined our staff to work with LHRAA as Administrative head.

Marlo Tellschow

On one occasion, I was invited to address a gathering of South Dakota pastors at a campsite on the west side of the state. I was to discuss with them the significance of selected Scriptural excerpts which might usefully inform ministries among people of Native American and tribal background. There were many facets of the two-day program that were specifically designed for feedback to church body personnel concerned with reservation and urban Indian affairs and life. So with expenses provided by those sponsoring offices I was able to ask Marlo to attend also and thus ensure a complete and coordinated report of presentations and discussions that emerged at the gathering.

Participants found the event profitable, and, at its close, a pastor from Rapid City, South Dakota, approached me, saying how much he wished members of his congregation might have heard my presentation. While I expressed my appreciation for his kind words, I told him travel plans had already been made for the rest of my stay there, making altered plans quite impossible. He left, and I became involved in conversation with others before they were on their way.

And then he returned. Like an efficient travel agent, he'd been checking on other travel options. He had found he could get a ride back with a fellow Rapid City clergyman so could leave his own Buick for me to drive into Rapid City, directly to his church. There he would have appropriate vestments waiting for me. He would do the liturgy and I would slip into the pulpit to deliver the sermon. From that point on, he would get me to the airport and my trip homeward. What could I say? He suggested the time I should leave, gave me the keys to the car, and said an appreciative "See you in the morning!"

The next morning, Marlo was at the car, waiting for me. We agreed to postpone getting some breakfast until we arrived at our destination. It was a gorgeous morning—beauty everywhere! This was the West—bright skies, uncluttered landscape. We saw huge rabbits; some deer too. And even a group of wild horses!

And after miles and miles of smooth riding, we at long last saw a large sign up ahead with this distressing message: *WELCOME TO WYOMING!*

Near panic!

We turned around immediately and lamented that for miles and miles, we'd not seen a store or gas station or anyplace that might have a telephone. Finally we spotted one and called the church where the pastor answered and learned of our plight. He chuckled, but assured us that if we pressed our accelerator, we could still make it. He would start the worship service without me and reserve a spot for me to squeeze in with a sermon.

As soon as we arrived, Marlo helped me slip on the vestments my host had laid out for me. I could see the pastor was serving the last group of kneeling worshippers their communion wine. The organist stopped her playing as the pastor led me into the pulpit. After I finished my sermon, eager not to prolong the service, the pastor prayed a quick dismissal prayer, pronounced the benediction and sent what surely must have been an amazed and probably weary flock of worshippers on their way.

In important ways, Marlo gave order to a complex agenda that refused to ease up through the years. On one particular morning in the busy spring of 1968, I was returning to my office, from an early class and found her at the door, phone in hand, waiting for me, whispering, "It's from NBC!"

It was Ted Elbert on the line, although most often an Elbert call was from his wife Joan, who was actively involved in the work of LHRAA's Chicago Chapter.

Ted Elbert.

Ted was a producer for NBC TV in Chicago. He was called on to cover such exciting events as the violent disorder at New York's Attica Prison, and later, the explosive experience of the Wounded Knee Reservation in South Dakota. He did European stories as well. In spite of the wide range of responsibilities for short-notice duties in distant places, Ted had a keen interest in LHRAA's ministry. And that's what had prompted this call.

The Church Federation of Greater Chicago had accepted the responsibility for supplying material for a weekly presentation in a nine-week series, titled *Everyman Speaks*. Its theme would be "Aspects of Black Power." Seeing an opportunity to involve LHRAA, Ted had told the planners that the organization might be able to put together a program that would help a Sunday morning audience understand and deal with the racial tensions of the day, providing voices of more militant blacks who would express their concerns and share their insights. While he was still telling his story, I was already trying to envision how we might respond.

In the previous summer, 1967, I had been invited to participate in a Walther League convention in Los Angeles. Some 150 young Lutherans were in the audience—most of them of high school age.

The program included a presentation by a man in his early forties, a member of the Black Panthers, an organization that had surfaced in California, giving voice to angry Black people protesting racist attitudes and actions. His name: Lenoir Eggleston, better known as Brother Lennie.

CHAPTER 16
BROTHER LENNIE

B rother Lennie was an artist with such talent that the renowned Diego Rivera had invited him to study and paint with him in Mexico until the master's death. When he returned to his home in Watts, (a Los Angeles community known for the explosive outbursts of racial violence there), Brother Lennie recognized the profound and painful sickness with which Los Angeles—and America—had become infected.

With a son in college and a daughter in high school, he resolved to set aside his love for art and dedicate all of his energy to giving his children a different kind of world and life. Now, working fulltime as a leader, coordinator, and organizer in his community, he was endeavoring to prepare Blacks—young and old alike—for a meaningful life.

Disenchanted with the irrelevance, indifference, and complacency of the institutional church, Brother Lennie had been invited to speak to these young people about his disdain for churches and the failure of Christianity to address the problem of racism. A member of and spokesman for the Black Panthers, he was both passionate and articulate in his role as an unchurched Black man bitterly unimpressed by Christianity as he saw it in the organized churches.

Because of his community involvement in Los Angeles, Brother Lennie had experienced fierce reprisal and even attempts on his life. He had been ruthlessly beaten by police. One episode resulted in a broken nose and a lacerated face, requiring stitches.

Clearly this was a man who had been an unusual participant in confronting racism, an artist turned activist.

My assignment on the program was to counter statements he would make that would be critical of the church's record on race relations.

On the day I was to be on stage with Brother Lennie, rather than disagree with any of his comments, I found myself expanding on some of the points he was making and noted that some of the comments the speaker had made were the very kind of concerns Jesus himself would have raised, even though they were not being spoken from many Christian pulpits.

The session closed with comments and questions from the audience. Among the first to speak were some voices raised to defend the church. Some spoke disparagingly of the comments their militant guest had made. Setting the tone for his remarks, Brother Lennie responded, "Don't put me down; I'm not going to put you down; that way, we can talk with each other." As the hour and a half session came to an end, the hall responded with loud, appreciative applause.

Before we parted, Brother Lennie and I had the opportunity for further conversation. He told me he'd never had occasion for the kind of dialog we'd had. He said he appreciated the experience and he made clear that he would hope for something like this to be repeated. "If ever you want to do something like this with me again, call."

Now, these many months later, as I was in conversation with Ted Elbert, the memory of that California experience flashed through my mind and I shared the story with Ted. Before our conversation came to an end, I had told him about Brother Lennie. We agreed to explore the possibility of arranging for our following through on the opportunity to participate in this TV venture.

My assignment was to contact Brother Lennie. He welcomed my call and agreed to come to Chicago, if his wife were included in our invitation. That was all that was necessary to begin our working out the details.

First, we had to plan a program that would fit into the frame of the *Everyman* TV series. The TV people suggested a format that would focus on Brother Lennie and his presentation. This would be followed by a response from a panel of four, preferably two Black, two White.

We contacted two Black clergymen who served Lutheran parishes on Chicago's South Side: Pastors Richard Dickinson and William Griffen. They agreed to participate. The other two places would be filled by Ted's wife Joan, at that time chairperson of LHRAA's Chicago Chapter—and me.

Problem: there were costs. We estimated that figure to be near $1,000 and there were no provisions for this project in LHRAA's modest and already strained budget. NBC was not going to pick up the tab, so appeals went out to LHRAA's Chicago Chapter, to George Hrbek who headed up our LHRAA Chicago Project (which at that time had headquarters on Chicago's South Side in "the Mansion,"), to Jim Cross of the Missouri Synod's Missions office, and to a handful of loyal friends of LHRAA as well as a few Lutheran congregations in the Chicago area.

We were so close to raising the amount needed that we also arranged for Pastor Fischer of Riverside Congregation on Chicago's far west side to have a program with Brother Lennie in the evening of our recording the *Everyman* telecast, with the anticipated offering designated to help meet our expenses. Everything started falling together and flight tickets were mailed to our invited guest.

End of story? Hardly.

Late in the day, Monday, April 22, a frantic Ted Elbert called to tell me we had trouble. Brother Lennie had landed. He had followed the instructions we had provided and had gone directly to the Bismarck Hotel, where Ted had reserved a room for him.

The clerk, sizing up this man—dressed somewhat unusually—no buttoned-at-the-neck shirt, no tie, carrying no suitcase, groomed somewhat hippyish, informed him they had no reservation for him and no rooms were available.

Frustrated and angry, Brother Lennie stormed to a telephone and called Ted. Hearing the story from Ted, I raced the sixty miles toward Chicago immediately—and by the time I arrived at the Elberts' home, things had calmed down. Joan had served a warm meal, which along with the family's hospitality, had engendered a cordial visit. The fever of the tense confrontation of the hotel incident had subsided and the Elberts graciously hosted the Egglestons in their home.

Brother Lennie said he'd like to see some of his "Black brothers" while here, and asked whether we knew any of them. Joan told him this story about Fred Hampton.

An ice cream truck had been making its way through a Black Chicago neighborhood. A bunch of kids started chasing the truck, begging for ice cream. When the driver told them to go away, they started pushing at the truck, rocking it back and forth. The driver began to be frightened. Both sides, ice cream man and the youngsters, were screaming at each other. Fred Hampton came along. When he realized what was going on, he opened the door of the truck and took out an ice cream bar for each of the kids and sent them on their way.

The merchant was angry about the driver's losses, but Fred had kept his truck from tipping and averted the possibility of igniting the beginnings of a small riot in that neighborhood.

In the very early hours of the next day, I was back in my own bed, weary, but relieved—and excitedly anticipating tomorrow.

The next day, we met at St Paul's Lutheran Church in suburban Melrose Park where Arthur Constein, the pastor, worked with us to do the filming of this telecast program at his church. We had a few hours for visiting together before we were scheduled next to be at Ascension Lutheran Church in suburban Riverside.

Brother Lennie had been impressed with the Hampton story. "Can you get Fred Hampton and some of his friends to come over so I can meet them?" he asked.

They came. He talked. They stayed. And they came along with us to the evening meeting at Ascension. After Brother Lennie finished speaking, he invited questions and comments from the audience.

One older man—apparently a long-time member of the congregation, stood up and acknowledged that some of the things Brother Lennie had said were harsh and not easy to hear.

"But," he said, "I really resent your having all those young Black men on the platform with you up there as bodyguards. This is a bit insulting to us. Do you think you are not safe here with us?"

Brother Lennie paused before he spoke. "How many of you would be willing to go alone to a Black church on Chicago's South Side tonight and be the only White person there?"

Once he left us, we were never able to contact Brother Lennie again. We heard reports that he had been assassinated.

We do know, however, that after Brother Lennie's visit, Fred Hampton himself became a Black Panther and that Fred was killed in a confrontation planned by law enforcement officers in Chicago. He was shot while in his bed, asleep. Police claimed they had been fired at first, from inside his bedroom. Their "proof" was a hole in the wall. In fact, however, newspaper reporters, who later examined the hole, confirmed that the "hole" was actually a nail hole. All bullets had been fired *into* his bedroom.

CHAPTER 17

THE ELLWANGER STORY

S hortly after enrolling at Concordia seminary, I learned of an extracurricular program offered there which introduced students to the experience of visiting with patients at a mental hospital on Arsenal Street on St. Louis's Southside. The program had been developed under the leadership of Pastor Walter Ellwanger, a Lutheran institutional chaplain. He was a warm, gentle pastor, understanding and caring. It was not too long after I had first met him that he was named President of a Lutheran elementary and high school for Negroes in Selma, Alabama.

He and Mrs. Ellwanger had three sons: John, who would become pastor of a church in Austin, Texas; Joseph, who became pastor of St. Paul Lutheran Church, serving an African-American community in Birmingham, Alabama (and later at Cross Lutheran Church in inner-city Milwaukee); and David, who studied law at the University of Alabama and later served in the highest level of administration of the American Bar Association in Los Angeles, later in Washington, D.C., and, after that, the national organization.

Joseph had lived in Alabama already in his youth. Now in his career role as a church leader, he became personally troubled by the racial confrontations that were daily surfacing in his Birmingham ministry and in his life with increasing intensity. Our Institutes at Valparaiso afforded him occasion for finding new supportive friends and encouragement for the role that was his in this difficult hour of history.

I had not met Joseph until he attended LHRAA Institutes on our campus. And, of course, he would be attending and participating in all of the human relations programs of our organization. In the years that followed, our visits together and phone calls have made the bonds of our friendship richer and stronger. He has become and remains a treasured colleague and friend.

Joe was unmarried then. At our Human Relations Institutes, we had opportunity to notice how young women in attendance found him to be attractive and engaging. I cannot remember that he and I ever even discussed his unmarried status back then. He was simply very absorbed in his intensely challenging Birmingham ministry.

These were the days when Black citizenry marched with tired feet across the South, holding high their protest signs, singing their freedom songs, saying "NO MORE!" to the oppressive shackles imposed by racial segregation. Black clergy of other denominations were affording leadership with their display of courage and commitment to the cause of removing the shackles of oppression from the ankles of a long abused people. The national media could no longer ignore the shameful tolerance that, for so long a time, had marked the culture and custom of demeaning the Black people.

Among the most impressive of such exposures was newscaster Howard K. Smith's hour-long TV program in his national network series, *Who Speaks for Birmingham?* I found this film particularly useful in my classroom presentation to students who, I discovered, were woefully ignorant of the severity of the brutish, vicious behavior to which these churchmen and their families were subjected. They were kicked and beaten, their homes and churches bombed and burned. And Birmingham, Alabama, had become a dramatic exposé of this bitter and explosive face-off.

Blacks had pledged themselves to non-violence. Racial attacks had reached the boiling point. Public officials and the police lost all control of the outbursts. They resorted to use of clubs, fire hoses, metal pipes, and fierce attack dogs in efforts to end the demonstrations once and for all.

For the most part, White churches in Birmingham (as well as White churches throughout the South) were reluctant to raise a prophetic voice against racial injustice, White supremacy, White superiority, White privilege.

Not the churches in the Black communities, however!

Pastors of these congregations spoke out from their pulpits and took to the streets their words of protest against the cruel and shameful patterns and practices that marked White society's relations with African-Americans. These churchmen took their stand in the face of hateful personal and physical abuse. In doing so, these courageous Black church leaders got to know Joe Ellwanger, this young White pastor at St. Paul Lutheran Church and regarded him an ally. They asked him to partner with them in their efforts. And he did.

Chris McNair, a young Black photographer, whose skills *TIME Magazine* recognized and would occasionally call upon, was a member of Joseph's congregation. On Sunday morning, September 15, 1963, as Chris was attending service at St. Paul, an usher disrupted his worship, directing him to leave at once. He rushed to the horrifying death scene at Sixteenth Street Baptist Church where Chris's little daughter, Denise, together with her three young classmates, Cynthia Wesley, Addie Mae Collins, and Carole Robertson, were killed by a delayed time bomb explosion that had been set to detonate at worship time.

In such an hour, outrage righteous indignation of African-Americans toward any and all White men would have been understandable. In addition, one understands the hostility toward the perpetrators of such a heinous and hateful crime, as well as to those White citizens and institutions that had tolerated and thereby nurtured the rotten seeds of racial arrogance through the years.

What the community did see, however, was Chris McNair on television, begging the community not to react with violence and thereby dishonor the memory of his child. And that afternoon, neighbors of those four little children would see Pastor Ellwanger on television, together with two courageous women of Birmingham's White citizenry—one, a Unitarian Universalist, the other a leader in the Jewish community. They would visit the home of each of those girls' families in an expression of love and care in this moment of the city's shame and these families' crushing grief.

The African-American clergy who provided leadership for organizing the civil rights demonstrations welcomed Pastor Joe as one of their own. White pastors, however, wished he would back off. Public figures in the White community disowned him and the most rabid of the racist-minded folk devised their own ways of harassing him. Joe told of fire trucks being dispatched to his address in the middle of the night and of an ambulance team at his door awakening him, explaining that they had been called to "pick up his body." It was to this Birmingham that this young White pastor would be returning each time we would have been together.

* * * * *

We tried whenever possible to have our LHRAA Board meetings in larger cities where there would be Lutheran churches whose leaders wanted to be supportive of the kind of ministry in which we were engaged. We would schedule our actual meeting time for Friday afternoons and the Saturdays that followed. On the Sunday mornings at worship time, the Board members and staff would fan out to these churches and speak in worship services.

On one occasion, our Washington, D.C., LHRAA members had made all of the arrangements for such a visit/Board meeting. On the next morning—a Sunday—Lutheran congregations in the vicinity heard our messages, emphasizing the role of reconciliation assigned to the Christian community when interracial confrontations were so prevalent. After the church services, Joe and I said goodbye to the other Board members. The group dispersed to head for their respective homes.

Joe and I were both to leave from Washington National Airport so we shared a cab to get there.

Since my flight to Chicago and his to Birmingham were not leaving immediately, we agreed to have a cup of coffee together at the airport while waiting. He excused himself to call his brother David in Birmingham.

When he returned to our table, he was unusually pale. Then he explained. David, together with a fellow student at the Alabama University School of Law, had been in and out of the offices of the Mayor and the Chief of Police and they learned that the police had been informed of Joseph's travel plans and were intending to arrest him as he arrived in Birmingham.

Joe was stunned; this was surely nothing he had anticipated. And I was hardly the one to suggest decisions or offer wise counsel. We agreed, however, were he not to be on this flight, he would be buying some time to consider various ways in which the situation might unfold. So both of us exchanged our tickets for later flights, stepped into the airport restaurant and had dinner together.

Shortly after my arrival at home, Joe, as he had promised, called me and calmly reported his safe arrival. No formal reception had been provided by the police. We were both relieved that evening. We were well into the next day when Joe called me again. It had been a busy, unsettling morning for him. The police had brought Joe to the District Attorney's office.

They brought into the room a Black man of the streets who was "doing time" and was obviously very uncomfortable in this setting, probably frightened. The District Attorney took on the role of interrogator, and, pointing at Joe, asked the man, "Is this the man who talked to you and made sexual advances to you in the public toilets?" He nodded his head and assented. The man was then dismissed and sent on his way.

Then, addressing Joe, the D.A. told how his office had been receiving reports of Joe going into buildings with men — Black men—and staying inside with them for long periods of time. "And now we have the word of this fellow telling us that you had met with him in a public lavatory. So you see why we have to deal with those charges. What do you have to say for yourself?"

Joe responded that he had never met this man before and furthermore that he never used public restroom facilities.

As for his being seen with "Black men," he explained that he frequently met with Black clergymen. These men, after all, were the leaders who themselves shared the brunt of racial attacks. They knew and had experienced the history of years and years of brutality inflicted upon their parishioners and their forebears at the hands of White hate-mongers.

These Black pastors were from the ranks of those whose churches and parsonages had been set afire by ruthless racists. They remembered the recounting of stories of terror and lynchings; they had watched the flames and smoke rise from the fiery crosses blazing on a neighbor's lawn. They were joining hands to respond with support for each other in leading the people of their community to stand up against injustice and to do so in the spirit and manner of their Leader, Jesus Christ. Jesus surely would have stood tall denouncing racism in its many manifestations and in its devastating of human spirit, crushing of physical well-being. And Joe simply told them he had been accepting their invitation to walk with them, as together they would be planning non-violent demonstrations on behalf of interracial justice.

The officers then said, "It's your word against theirs; and that's what we've got to deal with in our office. But maybe we can help you. If you were to get in touch with your area church leaders and persuade them to assign you to be pastor of a different parish some distance away from here, we'd simply have no reason to follow up on the charges against you."

As soon as Joe could get to the phone, he called me to report on the morning. He was surely shaken by their incredibly shameful and conniving behavior. He hadn't yet decided what steps he would be taking. I offered my suggestion: "First, call the members of your congregation to tell them what happened and ask for their help in thinking the whole matter through; and then call some of the Black clergy who are your friends, and ask for their counsel."

Before the day was over, Joe called to report that members of St. Paul assured him of their respect and loyalty. They expressed shock that such accusatory and demeaning charges could ever be contrived against their pastor, a shepherd whom they had found to be so faithful and guileless. One White Lutheran Birmingham pastor, upon learning about what happened, and apparently assuming that young Ellwanger would surely accept the alternate "offer of escape," assured Joseph that the move to another position was altogether feasible, and he himself would see to it that such arrangement would be expedited.

The Reverend Herbert Oliver (who later was to become the Superintendent of Schools in New York City) was one of the Black clergy with whom Joe shared his story of the threatening ultimatum. He told how a situation similar to this had happened some months earlier also in Birmingham. A White pastor of another denomination had spoken out against segregation. He too had been threatened and, under the guise of being helpful, the government officials offered the same kind of "avoiding the confrontation" by the same "escape route" they were now offering Joe.

Circumstances for that man and his family were such that he had not felt he had the support to follow through by taking the heroic stand. The Black clergy simply said they weren't in a position to condemn that man for deciding to leave the scene, but they assured Pastor Ellwanger of their support, should he choose to stay on and resist the ploy. There was a clear pattern of attempted intimidation that could be traced—and faced. And, indeed, Pastor Ellwanger was never contacted on the matter again.

Joe had been involved with LHRAA for over ten years when the incidents described above began developing in the early 1960s. He had found supportive and encouraging allies in the LHRAA's personnel and in our programs. He in turn proved to be a tremendously important resource for LHRAA staff. Early on, he was named a member of the Association's Board of Directors.

The strength and effectiveness of LHRAA's ministry increased as people who attended our Institutes would leave those gatherings with renewed commitment. They would win more support for our work in their home communities. These were not simply names on a roster of members. Our mutual and shared commitment to removing the wall of racial division resulted in the forming of strong friendships among us.

In this setting, Joseph got to meet a wonderful young woman from Kansas who became Mrs. Joyce Ellwanger. Theirs was a marvelous partnership. They shared faith, vision, perspective, commitment, and courage, and a love for the people they served as well as a selfless love for each other.

The Ellwanger's parsonage was hardly a Taj Mahal. Family income was blushingly meager, but together Joe and Joyce had made it an inviting, hospitable, and welcoming place. I would often be a guest in their home. It seemed appropriate, while assessing their situation, to take note of their transportation.

On one of my visits to Birmingham, Joe met me at the airport. He was driving a Mercedes Benz. Joe had lived modestly with minimum resources needed for his bachelor life. One could hardly begrudge him such a status symbol. Since the car's engine seemed a bit louder than I had expected, I ventured the guess that perhaps the car's muffler deserved some attention.

Joe chuckled a bit as he explained that the car was an older model and operated on diesel fuel. He also stated that it had been driven by a series of previous owners before it became his. In short, it was a rather tired car. "But," he added, "It still works!"

By this time, Joe and Joyce had not only become parents; they were extremely close to doing an encore. As Joyce put it, "Any time now!" In deference to Joyce, we agreed to retire at a reasonable hour and postpone the further exchange of stories till breakfast time.

It must have been one o'clock or so when my door opened—it was Joe.

He whispered that the birthing signs had begun and he needed to take Joyce to the hospital immediately. "Will you take care of the little one sleeping in our bedroom next to your door? He's a sound sleeper, but there's milk in the refrigerator, should he wake. We'll keep in touch."

Their car was parked on the side of the house near my window. I heard their anxious voices but wasn't able to discern any of the words. Joe started the car. The engine growled a bit, and then all was silent. He gave it another try. Nothing happened. Joe tried again. As the engine coughed a bit, it once again failed. Then, as if wanting to give it a last desperate try, the Mercedes came to life and stilled all our anxious hearts.

Bottom line: healthy new arrival; triumphant mothering; relieved father; and visiting babysitter; all of us grateful; and lots of thanksgiving prayers.

CHAPTER 18

THE MARCHES AND DEMONSTRATIONS

The Albany March – Georgia, August 28, 1962

Probably the most sobering of these marches for the LHRAA staff was prompted by an invitation to our office from Dr. Martin Luther King, Jr. in 1962.

Dr. King had sent the identical correspondence to clergy people in New York, Detroit, and a few other metropolitan centers of the North. His purpose was to gain support for his non-violent movement against racial segregation.

It was the busy, tension-packed mid-summer of 1962. The Black leader was inviting like-minded church leaders in the North to stand with the Black citizens of Albany, Georgia, supporting them in their efforts to register to vote. In the twelve preceding months, more than 1,000 Black citizens of Albany had made their way to the voter registration office, only to be denied and carried off to jail. To be released, each had been made to pay $200, a staggering investment in freedom made by a near impoverished community.

In promoting this demonstration Dr. King was hoping to gain the involvement of clergy persons of as many religious denominations as possible in an action that would capture the attention of reporters and television cameras from all across the country. The unusual event was intended to be a statement of demonstrated concern for fellow citizens of the South who were being denied their basic human rights, simply because they were African-American. Back home, members of the respective church bodies would surely see how committed their leaders were in expressing their moral indignation at the attitude of tolerance for persistent blight of segregation that had become the African-American's scourge and the nation's shame.

Andrew Schulze and I immediately realized the responsibility that was ours to assure Lutheran support for the plan. When Valparaiso's President Kretzmann heard of our decision to be involved, he called to assure us of his support for our intentions to participate in the event.

Members of Dr. King's staff were pleased with the promise of our participation and notified us of a briefing meeting to be held in the Chicago area the following Saturday.

Our calendar for those weeks was already crowded with commitments to meet with various individuals and groups to support them in their own confrontations with racial problems in their locale. We agreed that one of us should go as participant in the trip south and the other would stay behind to "mind the store."

When Saturday arrived, he and I—and Mrs. Schulze, too—drove to Chicago for the preparation session. Andrew Young and another of Dr. King's team were on hand to make sure we understood the physical and mental dangers that lay ahead for participants. The preparation included demonstrations of how to cover one's head and in other ways protect oneself when physically attacked. They explained the principles of non-violence and non-retaliation. And they would not be offended should any who volunteered to go along south choose to withdraw.

Andrew Schulze was not in his strongest health at this time and I offered to go south on the bus with the other clergy folk from the Chicago area. Andrew's response: "No, Karl, I've been writing and speaking on all this for years and now that I'm faced with the challenge to be standing up and be counted, I cannot walk away." We both looked at Margaret, his wife, who, without a word, nodded her assent and support. In her quiet support of Andrew, she showed her own determination and strength.

Andrew and Margaret Schulze

A few days later, we were in Chicago again, this time to see Andrew and his friends board the chartered bus to Albany, Georgia. The mood of the participants, as well as that of their loved ones, who had brought them to this place of departure, was sober. All of us were quite familiar with reports of the brutal, physical harm that others had experienced in demonstrations elsewhere. No banners had been pasted to the sides of the bus. Windows were closed. No singing of *We Shall Overcome* or any of the "freedom songs."

The focus of these visitors was to spell out, by their presence, their commitment to stand at the side of these courageous people of Albany, who have been seeking for their neighbors, their children, and themselves the rights God would have them enjoy for a full life that was rightfully theirs as citizens of this country.

Albany Chief of Police, Laurie Pritchett, assumed a unique role in what, in many respects, brought a touch of pageantry to the event. As the busload of church folk arrived at the outskirts of Albany, they were stopped by two policemen who escorted the visitors to homes in the Black community for the night.

The next morning, the northerners appeared on the sidewalk outside the county courthouse. As if the script for what was happening had been written beforehand, Chief Pritchett, neatly groomed for the occasion, addressed the group, asking, "Why are you here?"

There had been no spokesman appointed for this confrontation. A rabbi in the group spoke up: "We have come here to pray."

In commenting on this reply later, Andrew said, "I suppose any one of our group would have answered Pritchett's question differently, but I myself was so nervous, I'm sure I was praying. And I'm sure all my companions who were standing with me were praying too."

Pritchett resumed lead-man role, ordering these northern church folk to disband, return to their pulpits up north, and tend to problems there. And when these church folk did not comply, they were arrested. These people had in a quiet, orderly way and with dignity, presented themselves as faithful friends of people who had been victims of continued abuse and injustice. They were taken to jail. Among the charges: disorderly conduct. One of the women travelers stepped aside so she would not be arrested. She provided contact and communication with the sponsoring church groups in the North, apprising them of what was happening to their confined partners.

The little county jail was hardly able to accommodate this sudden spillover of residents. Neighboring county jails helped out. And when all available beds were put to use, pallets were brought in for excess inmates' use.

It was in these hours that Valparaiso University's President Kretzmann sent a message to President Kennedy, urging him to bring the involvement of his office to support efforts to rid the country of systems of segregation that stain our image as a democratic nation.

The incarcerated church leaders were reluctant to speak much of their days of imprisonment. Andrew put it this way, "Karl, what we are experiencing here is just a few hours, a few days. The people of Albany have had to live under this cloud of suppression and fear day after day for years. It is they who are the survivors, the heroes, rather than the few of us who tasted its ugliness for such a short time and then left again."

Andrew spoke a bit about the filth of the jails, the roaches and other bugs and the stench. He told too of the night that the two not-so-friendly jailers came into their cell with two very large and very drunk Negro men and told them, "Look at all these people lying here, half asleep; they're all White preachers and they came here because they love colored people, so get them up and give them all a hug!" Andrew explained that the two men were really frightened by the situation. The clergy got up and walked over to meet the two inebriates and embraced them. This angered the two officers who then left, taking the two arrestees with them.

The jailed visitors from the North returned to their sleeping spots. Theirs had been a long day. They were hardly back to sleep, however, when the two jailers and their charges returned. This time, they ordered the men to urinate on the clergy. Of course they were reluctant, but this was the South.

Each day we were receiving reports on how the demonstrators were faring. I would call President Kretzmann to apprise him of what we were learning. One morning, his secretary, Mrs. Heidbrink, called me to his office. She lifted her large desk blotter and retrieved an envelope containing ten twenty dollar bills (not a University check!) so that Andrew could be released from his cell.

Later, when he was back at his desk in our office, Andrew would often recall his Albany experience. He counted those days as some of the most important in his entire life. He recalled the celebrative "thank you service" that the Black community held upon his release and their expressions of gratitude.

And of course there were letters of commendation and appreciation from fellow Lutherans for his demonstration of courage and faithfulness.

There were also letters from a few Lutheran people who resented his "poor judgment, his disappointing conduct, and thoughtless action."

Andrew had begun having health problems, but he said he was always aware that his Lord was with him and his stay in Albany had been endurable because of that assurance.

At one of our LHRAA Board meetings—this one in St. Louis—and after a wrap-up session in one of the churches, we were prepared to travel to St. Louis's Lambert Field, where we would be catching our flights to our different home sites.

It had been a good meeting, so we were hardly prepared for a hurried announcement by one of our local hosts, who had stood to thank us for coming and to apprise us of expressions of sincere appreciation of our visit by the St. Louis host churches. He then told how in this very hour, the local radio stations had reported a march getting underway heading to the heart of the city, commemorating the death of a civil rights worker.

One of our group rose to say, "There always seem to be people who regard marchers as trouble makers. In our *VANGUARD,* we've always reminded our readers of the official statement of our government, assuring us that it shall be the right of people to 'peacefully assemble' in the redress of grievance. This would be an opportunity to endorse and affirm such a stand."

Not only did we all stay on four more hours to join in the demonstration, but we found ourselves being photographed by the *St. Louis Globe-Democrat*'s Paul Ockrassa assigned to cover the event for his paper. Paul identified himself as Lutheran. He said he was so very surprised to find a group of Lutherans participating in this display of interracial concern. With that, he handed his camera to a co-worker and joined us in the march.

The March on Washington—August 28, 1963

LHRAA's relationship with Valparaiso University President Kretzmann was encouraging and supportive. He often called us to be updated on our activities. He became especially intrigued as we learned more and more about the hurdles and complications that planners and conveners of the event faced as they were anticipating the launching of what was long to be remembered as the awesome, historic "March on Washington."

I told him of LHRAA's efforts to enlist Lutherans to join in the procession of marchers, lest we be seen as people unsupportive of those seeking to remove the shackles from the ankles and wrists of victims of segregation and racial injustice and that I had already made most of my plans to be there for the event.

He was pleased.

And then he asked, "I'd really appreciate it were you to take my oldest son with you. I would hate for him to miss it, but I also would appreciate his having an escort." I knew Jody very well—he went to high school with Peter, our eldest son. So that was an easy favor.

This march itself was breathtakingly phenomenal, spearheaded by long-time civil rights leader, A. Philip Randolph, renowned union organizer of the Pullman (railway) Porters. He enlisted the support and involvement of others for this event that he had magnificently coordinated. The participation of national civil rights leaders with Martin Luther King's Southern Christian Leadership Conference, the National Urban League, the National Association for the Advancement of Colored People, and the Congress of Racial Equality.

We arrived in the nation's capital and immediately went to Peace Lutheran Church. There was no sermon. Pastor Herbert Schwandt chose some psalms to read and collects to pray for a day of humility and prayer. They were short, sobering readings and particularly meaningful Scriptures. After each reading, the pastor paused for three or four minutes. The church remained completely silent as the congregation meditated on the words just read.

This was a serious event. This was no lark. No one talked of danger or of anything going wrong, but everyone knew that something could go wrong and could do inestimable damage to the cause that the demonstrators had embraced. Never had there been this kind of gathering before: two hundred and fifty thousand people; Black hands and White hands together.

Participants holding their signs up high were identified as "Lutherans marching" and with LHRAA. The authorities had not known what to expect. Police and military personnel were everywhere. Their presence was at once reassuring and superfluous. The New York Times described the mood as that of a church picnic. Never had such considerateness by March participants been seen before. Had anyone wanted to push ahead—and none did —that person would have been helped. No one would have shouted "down in front" to someone who blocked another's view. Actually, people were so concerned about

LHRAA at "March on Washington."

others that they were making every effort to see that they would not be obstructing someone else's line of vision.

As five and six hours wore on—and speech after speech—and the sun was hot and shade was sparse—it might have been expected that people would grow tired and irritable. Tired, yes, but not irritable. On the long walk back and on the highway 1,500 buses, countless cars, waving, helpfulness, smiles everywhere. These people had joined in the common cause.

Oh, the speeches were monumental, the program of highest caliber. But the huge throng of Americans was at the foot of Lincoln's image and was dedicated to the task of making this the great nation for which people have died. This will never be forgotten.

Letter to My Family in Sheboygan

And when I got home again, I put the following words together in a letter to my sisters and parents back in Sheboygan, Wisconsin.

> *Hello – I spent the night in Baltimore after agreeing to meet with other Lutherans there. I have just now boarded a plane for Washington where I got on another flight to Charlotte after a four hour layover there and then jumping on another plane for Pensacola, Florida. The Millers (Caroline and Bob) will join us and four others in a serious meeting to explore ways to crack the hard South. I am scheduled to be back in Chicago Saturday noon.*

Yesterday was a great day. Some 350 Lutherans from all over the country were gathered together to participate in the "March." It was nothing short of thrilling. Over 200,000 people—this is alone an overwhelming thing. But the orderliness, dignity, considerateness, harmony, and unit—the devoted and serious commitment—that marked the occasion were something to behold. When could you be in any crowd where there is not some pushing and shoving, elbowing for better vantage and view? The courtesy and warmth—even with spectators—was nothing short of amazing.

And the Lincoln Memorial as backdrop to the event had all kinds of thrilling implications. While we Lutherans were beginning our part in the March to the Washington Monument from Mt. Olive Lutheran Church, where we had just had a service (there had been another the night before) a cab stopped for another clergyman to jump out and join us. One Elmer Witt! Dr. Harms (then Synod President) had told the press "the Lutheran Church – Missouri Synod will not be represented." Well, there may have been no official appointment or assignment, but we were there – strong.

Bill Kohn, recently elected full time president of the Southeastern District, (LCMS) marched with us. He has come a long way in his feelings in all this! And he said "I am proud of these Lutherans." The closing words read by the pastor who led our service had been "Little children, let us not love only in words or speech, but in deed and in truth!"

We filed from the church singing "Onward Christian Soldiers . . . with the cross of Jesus going on before." And as I turned around I saw in the rear pack of marchers a young lady—Caroline Roberts Shephard! I had baptized her in Muskogee when she was just a child, confirmed, and married her. She had spent a year at Valpo too and she had been our organist in Muskogee. She said she remembered how after closing vacation Bible school sessions back in Oklahoma all of us used to sing "Onward Christian Soldiers" as we'd send the little children down the sidewalkless, unpaved streets to their segregated ways of life. And she always had felt that White people—and the rest of the Lutheran Church—never particularly cared. Now a resident in DC herself, she was deeply moved to see this significant participation.

The stories and vignettes stack a mile high. Hundreds of Zacchaeuses were perched in trees along the way. For all of us there, what a great historical experience! "Of the people, by the people, for the people" took on new meaning for our country yesterday. Thanks for your prayers.

Love to all of you.
Karl

White Man's Demonstration, Selma, Alabama— Saturday, March 6, 1965

Already in my first meetings with Joseph Ellwanger I found him to be a genuinely humble, insightful, honest, courageous, deep, and committed servant of God. I made it my intent to be visiting or in communication with him as often as possible. He became my teacher, my consultant, my companion. And, I had hoped, I might fill that kind of role and be the same kind of friend to him.

The early days of March, 1963, helped me realize how strong those ties between us were. For several weekdays, he'd been calling me to share his plans for a significant event he had wanted to undertake.

It was obvious that a large number of White citizens of Alabama deplored the segregating practices that characterized the lives of Black people in the South. It would seem difficult and dangerous for White southerners to publicly stand up and be counted as opponents of the segregated system. However, Joe had already found a group that met monthly, identifying themselves as White southerners who were against the southern culture of White superiority.

Joe had invited the group to accompany him on a demonstration to the Dallas County Courthouse in Selma, Alabama, on behalf of Blacks who sought, but were denied, the right to register as voters. On March 5th, seventy-two of these good people indicated their willingness to participate in the event. Other than Joe himself, there were only two Lutherans who chose to be there—a

Lutheran minister to the deaf, Pastor Ervin Oermann (who at one time had been a Seminary student/intern in the parish I served in Oklahoma) and Joe's wife, Joyce who, as the Scriptures would put it, was "great with child."

Joe called me, explaining his readiness, asking whether I saw anything in his plan that needed attention. He asked me, should he first call the President of his district to apprise him of the march. My response: "Joe, this is your decision; you do not ask for permission to do what is God-pleasing. Why don't you instead call him, inviting him to participate with you, knowing he would surely want to join you in helping those trying to do what is right and good."

Joe did call him. After doing so, he reported back to me on the conversation. Dr. Homrighausen had been caught a little bit by surprise and told him he'd have to think that over until morning.

When the seventy-two White Alabamans—without President Homrighausen—all arrived at the appointed church, they walked in twos all the way—and quietly—to the courthouse steps, where they were met by sheriff's deputies who read to them a copy of a telegram they received that very morning from Dr. Homrighausen, insisting that the presence of these people had not been authorized by the church leaders.

The demonstrators sang "America, the Beautiful." Some two hundred spectators nearby played the role of distruptor and sang a few choruses of "Dixie." The Chief of Police, Wilson Baker, quietly urged Joe Ellwanger's group to take a different route back to the church. He would endeavor to assure their safety.

Joe had effectively forced an official leader of Lutheran churches of the South to expose the church as unwilling to stand by Blacks in their efforts to experience full citizenship in our country.

The Edmund Pettus Bridge Event
Selma, Alabama
Sunday, March 7, 1965

Staff members of the Southern Christian Leadership Conference (Dr. King's organization) had invited concerned people from all over the country to join them in a march from Selma to Alabama's capitol in Montgomery, to plead the rights of Negroes. Some 600 marchers—including women and children—followed two SCLC staff persons, who took the lead walking in two columns across the Edmund Pettus Bridge.

Law enforcement men appeared on the scene and ordered the marchers to turn back and to do so in two minutes. Thirty seconds later, not the full minute, the officers attacked—some mounted on horses, all of them lashing out at the frightened, panicking, and confused victims. Some police were wildly swinging baseball bats and night sticks; some wielded long pieces of metal pipe. Others used cattle prods, some tear gas, and all this against an eerie background of groans, screams, and sobbing while the "officers of the law "attacked them and forced them back across what came to be known as the "Bloody Bridge."

Those actions were filmed and shown on TV. Public outrage was spontaneous. Recognizing the need for harnessing the widespread righteous anger generated by Sunday's clash on the Pettus Bridge, Dr. King (and "all the King's men"—and women!) spoke words of invitation largely to the people of the churches to join them on "Turn Around Tuesday," to bespeak their solidarity with the beaten and bruised marchers ("martyrs!") of Sunday afternoon's shameful, brutish actions.

March from Selma to Montgomery, Alabama
Tuesday, March 9, 1965

By Monday morning, chartered planes, loaded busses, and countless rental and private cars filled the roads to Selma. By noon, all space in motels had already been reserved and local residents were helping to find lodging accommodations for these out-of-towners—clergy, nuns, union leaders, political persons, media people, rabbis, community leaders, and more.

When the call for enlisting further support had been sent out, it was, of course, important that many different corners be heard from, and especially that better known and more widely recognized names of participants be picked up to state the reasons for their participation.

The best name we could come up with, of course was LHRAA Board member, Pastor Joseph Ellwanger. He was already known for his role as a White clergyman, a champion of African-Americans in their struggle for human rights. People of the press would recognize him and he'd represent our Association well should any news people choose someone for interviewing.

I wondered whether we could identify some other prominent Lutheran leader whom we might enlist for the role. Clearly Martin Marty, Managing Editor of the respected *Christian Century* fit that description. I called him that Sunday evening. He hesitated for only a moment before assuring me that he welcomed the opportunity to express in person such matters that he often was obliged to express in writing.

Choosing him proved to be a good move. We did not see any printed words ascribed to him in any of the newssheets that ran stories on the happenings of these hours. However, we were told a Canadian TV program did a 20-minute production of a fine assessment of the Selma situation, calling on Dr. Marty to report on and to interpret the happenings in Selma this week.

Enlisting Dr. Marty to go to Alabama encouraged us to sign up an additional person to represent LHRAA in Selma. This prompted us to consider the name of another renowned Lutheran scholar whom reporters would recognize as a prominent Lutheran figure for interviewing. Listeners would surely take note that the Lutherans were supportive of the marchers. Our choice: Dr. Jaroslav Pelikan of Harvard University. To sign him up for the role seemed a shoo-in! (After all, his son, Marty, was a friend of my eldest son, Peter.)

One could understand the difficulty of organizing that had fallen into the lap of those who had originally designed the march from Selma to Montgomery: different groups arriving at different times, multiple meetings, revising of plans, miscommunications, altering of schedules, mixed messages, an estimated 3,000 people on hand, most of whom had never before been in Selma.

When I finally did reach the Pelikan home, Jarry was genuinely pleased to know we were including him as an ally in this historic moment. However, he reluctantly begged off. He had a busy week of pre-commitments that at this late hour couldn't be altered.

I could readily understand. At the very moment I was calling him, I was in my hotel room in St. Louis, about to leave for an hour and a half session with LCMS President Oliver Harms, to be followed by all-day planning meetings with church staff officers in sessions already scheduled weeks earlier, vital to the church body's response to the rash of problems that were sprouting in different locales across the country.

Half an hour later, I entered Dr. Harms' office. I steered the course of the conversation to Scripture passages that call for Christians to stand in defense of those who champion the cause of the poor, who speak up on behalf of those who have been silenced, or those who simply looked "the other way"—away from acknowledging the ingrained customs and practices that threatened the future of Black youngsters – infants to those of college age.

We talked about developing patterns of thought and planning programs to help congregations and their leaders to become partners with and supporters of people like Joe Ellwanger and his colleagues in Selma that very day.

Many times during the day, I thought about the good people in Selma, wondering if my place shouldn't be in Alabama.

And maybe in the office of Dr. Harms is exactly where I *should* have been right then rather than standing with the courageous marchers in Selma.

* * * * *

By Tuesday afternoon, the marchers had regrouped, and once more headed for the infamous bridge. With the two clergymen, Martin King and Ralph Abernathy, in the lead, the marchers (their numbers now swollen to 3,000!) resumed their unfinished march. Quite suddenly, the long column of walkers came to a standstill as those two stopped and knelt in prayer. They rose from prayer and turned the procession around to return to the church from which point the march had started.

The Montgomery Event
March 25, 1965

In the days and hours that immediately followed, it seemed to some that the vehicle had stalled. Some of the visitors had to return to their posts. But, no! The engine was idling while experts were tending to fine tuning. For instance, there was a meeting of 15 church leaders with President Lyndon Johnson. Joe Ellwanger was there.

A significant development involved a bit of sensitive negotiating with Federal Judge Frank Johnson. He arranged for the resumption of the march (on March 16) of the 600 original Marchers-to-Montgomery and assured federal protection for the remaining 48 miles of the long hike to Montgomery. This last phase was to culminate with sympathizing demonstrators who wanted to participate in the climax of this momentous event.

I called my wonderful, thorough, efficient, resourceful, and imaginative travel agent to secure transportation to get me to Montgomery. No flights, no trains, no rental cars—not even school busses; nothing was available to get me there. I was almost prepared to settle for a motorized golf cart.

And then a call from Valparaiso University's President Kretzmann informed me of his learning that forty of our students had driven to Montgomery, Alabama, and were already there to participate in the final leg of the march from Selma. All the news reports that morning had focused on the brittle nature of the event, expected to be the largest demonstration ever to have been brought into the South. He said "This could be horribly explosive." An estimated 15,000 people were expected to be there participating. He wished that some faculty from our campus would be there. He asked if I would be willing to take on that responsibility. He was concerned that our students might well be in far more serious danger than they realized.

I told him that all my attempts to get to Montgomery on March 25th finally had been thwarted, but I would keep trying to get there. Moments later, a friend called me from St. Louis to inform me that a group of priests and nuns there had chartered an out-of-use United Airlines plane for a flight to Alabama. It was a retired DC3, often affectionately called "a bucket of bolts," rugged and much used in World War II.

One seat was still not spoken for and I quickly committed myself as the last person to sign on. In spite of the bumpy ride, we made good time and landed at the Montgomery airport.

It was a gloomy day, no friendly airport personnel on hand to welcome us. No busses or cabs were available. No people were there to tell us where we should be going or how we were to get there. Finally, a tired-looking gray bus rolled toward us, its large blue letters identifying it as belonging to a local Baptist Sunday School.

The tall, Black driver stepped out and motioned his invitation to climb aboard. He must have assumed we had come to join the March. He told us where we were to "hitch on" to the procession which had already begun, the head of which was stretched out blocks beyond the place where we were.

The streets were lined with local citizens to watch the long procession—a strange blend of White people, some of them waving confederate flags, who were fearful of these White visitors as they regarded them as invasive trouble-makers and the Black people, many of them holding American flags, watching and grateful that some people were brazenly standing at their side as brothers and sisters.

By the time our "tail-end" of the lengthy procession arrived, those who had preceded us were already gathered in congenial groups, awaiting the rest of us who were still coming. I was amazed, early on, to locate all 40 of the Valparaiso students, and was not a little surprised to find my oldest son, Peter, among them. He had not mentioned to his mother or to me his plans to ride along with some of his campus friends. I found them among great numbers of people who were already gathered in the wide area that normally was used as parking space for Governor George Wallace and other government employees.

Each male marcher was asked to walk on the curb-sides of each line of seven persons across. This was to protect marchers on the interior in the event of attack. But President Kretzmann had been right in assessing the situation. That night, when the crowd was dispersing, the car in which Viola Liuzzo of Detroit was driving Black marchers was ambushed and she was murdered.

The next lines are words of mine that I wrote for LHRAA's VANGUARD while the excitement of the event was still fresh in my mind. They show my response to the experience of participating in the Montgomery March.

VANGUARD : Vol. 12 No.3 May 1965

"AND WE'RE GLAD WE WENT. . . "
by Karl Lutze

Waving families in the Negro community on porches and on curbings . . . Mothers with their babies on laps, children, grand-fathers, and great-grandmothers. And occasionally youth would spring from the porches with the encouragement of their elders: "Go on, boy!" "Run along with them, child."

And there were those instances when adults joined the ranks. Two mothers handed their babies to grandmothers and walked in beside us. They waved proudly to their friends on the side who smiled and cheered them on. One said, "My 15 year-old is in these lines and I intend to be with her. . . "

And suddenly at the side of us as we marched, appeared an old grandfather holding the hand of a little brown-skinned 4 year-old. They walked along for a block and then dropped out as the old man picked up the lad and spoke to him tenderly, "You marched, boy—you were in the great march . . . "

Old men and women wept . . . some sang along the freedom songs with the marchers. Some called out "Thank you, thank you . . . sing louder!"

There was Loveless School on our right —a misnomer—for there was obvious welcome and love as the children were dismissed from their classes to see the fantastic sight of people marching and demonstrating the song they sang "Black and White together . . . we shall overcome." And some adults called out "Children, you're in school—this is your history class."

As we moved on we came to a different neighborhood – different not only because the faces were lighter. The friendliness and spirit of warm and enthusiastic welcome disappeared. The much touted southern hospitality had chilled. We sensed a restrained hostility. It was reassuring to hear the 'copters hovering back and forth over our lines. But the National Guardsmen on hand were there only to carry out orders. Their resentment was obvious. . . . for the rest of the march we were much aware of the inhospitable mood of White Montgomery. It proved to have been a good morale strengthener that we had first come through the west side of a Negro neighborhood.

On a few porches White people sat, smiling friendliness and in some cases waving and on occasion some Whites downtown gave guarded nods of approval as if to say – "We don't dare join but we're glad you're here."

As I spoke with the Black woman from Montgomery, someone yelled; "Go ahead, Reverend, kiss her!" And there were other comments.

Confederate flags flew from office building windows. One young man on the curb waved such a flag tauntingly at the

marchers prompting a young lady student from Maryland College (near St. Louis) to respond, "Did you get a new flag for Christmas?"

But the marchers seemed thoroughly and unanimously overwhelmed with disbelief to see the great Alabama flag atop the equal-sized Confederate flag flying high above the capitol's mighty dome.

The only American flags to face when the National Anthem was to be sung were those carried by the marchers.

On the way back to the church on Ripley Street we walked in groups down side streets. Truck loads of National Guardsmen—Alabamans all—committed to the discipline of soldiering and yet their coolness and contempt so often quite overt . . . We paused and asked them and the state troopers who stood near. "Where is the First Baptist Church?" None of the cafés or eating establishments was open and we had heard that Black churches had pooled their resources and were serving food to the demonstrators.

[One of these uniformed officers stood about] 4 feet away and yet he made as if he didn't hear. So walking up to face him, we asked the words once more. He looked away and said, "I wouldn't know."

[I remember another policeman on a motorcycle. Each time I would ask that same question of him he would twist the handles of his steering gear, revving up his engine so that my words were completely drowned out.]

We found the church one block farther on . . . And we found love and welcome and more food than needed for a small army. We ate well. Chicken, casserole, potato salad, coffee, fruit dish and 2 oranges for the way. No suggestion for a fee or offering.

A woman in the kitchen said it this way: "We know how much White men can hate. Our church was bombed a few years ago. . . "There was a day when those of us who wished the best for our children tried to move, or at least send our children to the north to have a better life. No More. This is our home: our roots are here. We want our children to be educated and have a chance to make their home and live their lives here in a climate of peacefulness and dignity, of freedom and citizenship.

"We want the whole world to know it can't happen without big changes: and in this great country the changes are happen-

ing. You helped us tell the world today and
that's why we're so joyful and so grateful."
And we're glad we went."

As we left, the thickening, blackish clouds were gathering
and we found the crowd dispersing a bit hurriedly. As
soon as our group had found our seats on the plane,
our pilot announced his readiness for an immediate
departure.

The plane's engines screamed as we lifted from the
runway and we were airborne. We were on our way—a
good bit relieved that the man at the controls was a skilled
veteran flyer who insisted we stay strapped in our seats;
we were in tornado territory. No one doubted that.
Already doors to the overhead racks had jarred loose and
blankets, pillows, and other items had fallen out. Our
flight attendant, a long-time stewardess for United
remained in her seat, her seat belt fastened. She apolo-
gized for any discomfort we might have had and added,
parenthetically, that in all her years of flying, she
had never encountered the likes of what we were experiencing.

The passengers weren't indulging in clever conversation or in tongue-in-cheek comments of bravado. The
crescendo of clicking sounds from the "Sisters' Section"
assured us that rosaries had been called into action. One
elder nun in reverent seriousness prayed aloud, "Lord,
you know I'm always ready to tread all paths you have
walked, but please don't give Governor George Wallace
the satisfaction of gloating over my end coming as a result
of my taking part in this March opposing segregation."

When the plane had landed, taxied to the gate, and its engines had been silenced, the pilot, who had performed so valiantly, stepped out of his cabin. A look of relief and a broad smile crossed his face, while all of us passengers applauded him wildly.

And one of the priests commented, "Look at his white hair! Wasn't it brown when we took off this morning?"

Probably every one of the thousands who walked the streets of Montgomery that day had a personal story to tell. Our eldest son, Peter, who had been with the forty-plus Valpo students who made the trip wrote this message and presented it at the University Matins Worship.

Matins, Tuesday April 6, 1965
(Peter Lutze's Story)

It would be really neat, yeah, neat, to go down to Montgomery. Neat's the only word for it. I could hardly wait.

It was quite stirring when we said good-bye here—the martyrs leaving behind sweatshirts, pin-curls, and drooping half-awake eyes, leaving behind all that Valpo means. It might have been smoother if Blado hadn't had to run all over with Berryman's cup of coffee. But the kisses and the blessings fell and there was a tear or two. We turned and grabbed our swords and shields and steering wheels and set forth on our crusade to freedom. Freedom. Thank goodness we're going back down so when we get back we'll know what it means.

SUE: And I knew as I was leaving that I was marching for all those who couldn't be with us!

JINKY: Barbie and Grace had wanted to come so bad.

JIM: Bye, you guys; see you in three days.

The roads were snow and slick and ice and white and sliding and snow and ice and rain and slush and St. Louis. St. Louis was neat and we could hardly wait to get to the Sem, which was neat, too, so everybody'd heard. And it was neat at the "Sem"—except for when we all had to get out and push the car—and the buildings were sandy-colored, light bright solid reflections of a European heritage.

Somehow the hamburgers at Koiner's were burned and still were raw—and on raw-burned hamburgers, we set forth—not quite so nobly, but reinforced by ranks of neat seminarians—to the buses. The buses weren't ready or something and while they hulked huffily in the rain, we wandered bewildered into a church basement stuffed with whites, Negroes, pastors, ladies and college kids.

The sweatshirts and Levis of the world had not all been left in Valpo and long black hair, guitars and beards had been thrown in extra. We milled around and waited and milled around and read instruction sheets, milled around and finally following, pulled ourselves outside and plodded into the buses. It was darkening when we left St. Louis' rain and sleet. And we rocked on thru the night and sang the vespers with the squeaking windshield wipers.

JINKY: And some of these words took on new meaning somehow ...

ERNIE: *Blessed are the poor in spirit ...*

PETER: *He hath pulled down the mighty from their seats and exalted them of low degree.*

JUDY: *Yet all are one in Thee for all are Thine...*

CAROL: *Lord, have mercy upon us...*

It was even neater now, cuz the Sem students were really neat.

Birmingham was a 45-minute stop and an early springish morning and open windows and sunshine and Negroes waving on a street corner. Then Alabama countryside, red, clay soil and little hills of woods. A farm and house. It was green, too, and sorta neat.

Our driver must have been lost, 'cause we drove around Montgomery for fifteen minutes looking at Negroes, policemen, national guardsmen, and houses. We stopped at last in front of school, and even more bravely and nobly, too—for there was something in the air.

DONNA: Hey Kathy, do you believe we're really here?

We walked around behind it into an immense, muddy baseball field of people. People. And everywhere people; a monstrous circle stamped and moved and mingled, and sang—the raincoats and umbrellas and yellow muddy shoes and fluttering cardboard signs. It was hard, then at first, to sing, and there were a thousand things to see, but hesitantly we did begin. And we sang "O Freedom" and "Let My People Go" and "Song of Jubilee" and "He's Got the Whole World..."

Part of the circle began moving at last, the part up by the back gates, the part filled with knapsacks and glowing fuchsia vests. We waited and it was our turn to move out through the gates towards the street.

Six abreast, wc walked, then ran, then trotted, then walked through the mud onto gravel and into the street. It was a back street in the Negro section and people lined the road. We walked and ran a block and turned left and fat ladies waved at us and a toothless man. It was hard to wave back. But we waved. And marched down, then up.

The houses were gray and beat—losers to the elements, yet stubbornly, uncertainly standing. Yards were brown but for a few spots of grass and on the lawn stood and sat six year olds. They waved and sang the songs we sang, for we were singing now—and the first two blocks were the toughest. Their mothers sat on the porches and waved and clapped and said "Freedom" and sang "He's got the Whole World" with us.

We marched past a grubby filling station and a tattered store bespattered with a thousand ads and past some young men, too. Pastors on all sides and we sang as we walked up the hill through the slums of Montgomery.

RACHEL: They must have come all the way up from Selma...

ERNIE: *If you miss me at the back of the bus...*

DONNA: *And crown them good with brotherhood ...*

PETER: *Which side are you on, boys, which side are you on?..*

SUE: *How many times...*

We were smiled upon and blessed and we turned around at the top to a waving flood black and white and colors pushing up behind us. We walked on another block, faces, smiles, fat women sitting on unpainted porches, and a boy with a dog and a little brother on the broken steps of a tiny box.

We curved past a Negro school and we asked children hanging out the windows what they wanted. They said "Freedom" and they wanted it all now.

CAROL: When they're my age—things will be different for them...

It was hot, for the gray clouds pushed down hard and low. We bent around again past a national guardsman, down another block and another; past a sidewalk and a line of kindergartners singing with their teachers. And we walked and sang and it wasn't so hard to wave.

The boys walking beside the line told us not to break ranks, because we were entering the white part of town, just as eight Negroes beside the road held up two fingers in an old, yet new victory sign.

The houses improved, as did the yards—we passed two national guardsmen and their rifles and a state trooper at one intersection. And we curved and walked down the hill towards downtown.

"We shall Overcome..."

It was a little more hollow as we walked beneath the impassive staring faces in the second floor of a white, secretarial school. And yet a little more resounding and I twitched cold a moment in the 80 degrees. We walked now in the center of four lanes and there were very many marchers and the buildings were tall and gray.

A boy directing at the side held a small sign "Smile," and we walked into the middle of downtown Montgomery. The Jefferson Davis Hotel with windows open, and on an open porch, dark suits and ties and whiskey glasses in hands.

Negro maids and bellboys waved out the open windows and reaching up toward them, we waved. We waved, while on the sidewalks stood men in dark suits who watched thousands walk by. They stood in front of the hotels, not many and not interested. Just there and they stared at the waving crowd. Some shook their heads or smiled or mumbled but most stood with hands in pockets and watched the pounding sea flood past.

Past Newberry's, above whose street floor hung a black and white picture. And a circle around the head of a seated man and the words screamed "King at Communist School." We marched past Newberry's now and pushed harder for the road was turning up. White. Bright. Perfection.

At the top of the hill, way up there, far up there, above all the people, all the signs and all the bobbing American flags was the white capitol. The sky was blue and the capitol was a dome of white. St. Andrews cross— Alabama, and a red rag beneath it. A bloody Xed and starred rag. Trim and tiny and red against the sky. And it overshadowed the sky, the valley, the town, and us.

"Close up ranks! Close up. Move out. Keep up." We sang now, we sang hard and we sang. And my voice was hoarse and it cracked twice and we sang "We shall Overcome" and "God is on Our Side."

A white person ran three steps out into the street yelling, "God dam nigger lovah, get the ..."

"God is on our side today. Oh, oh, deep in my heart, I do believe..."

A red brick church—hurtin'—scraggled with locust trees beneath the shadow of the capitol, and Negro kids on the steps.

"Oh, oh Freedom, Oh, Oh, Freedom, OH-OH FREE-DOM OVER ME."

Here, we're here. Shout your lungs out—sing! We'd stopped and we sang now with the voices on the loud speakers. Ya gotta march when the spirit says march, ya gotta sing when the spirit says sing, ya got move when the spirit says move—on all sides of and past a stone marker— marching where Jefferson Davis had marched in the first inaugural parade of the Confederacy.

Sing! You'll never need that voice again, sing. And behind us—through and past and over Montgomery, they came, the endless roll of green raincoats, clericals, gym shoes, white shirts. Sweat and sore legs and burning faces and power pushed up the hill and Montgomery's buildings were tall and gray.

We stood, we sat, we stood, we listened, we ate, we sang "The Star-Spangled Banner," our national anthem. My shirt was sopped and it stuck to my skin and it began raining a little. We listened and listened and it took guts to listen to every local, state, and national civil rights leader who came before us.

JIM: Hey, you guys, there's Schaub...

PAUL: Ernie, are there any more oranges? ...

But we heard Shuttlesworth tear down that flag. He knew that what it said had been crushed beneath a boot a hundred years ago. We heard Mrs._____ mangle unmercifully the English language. And we heard King say, "Glory, glory hallelujah! His truth is marching on." And at least, finally we sang, "We Shall Overcome," with crossed, joined hands rocking in long rows. Thousands and thousands rocking in long rows between the tall state of Alabama office building, beneath the binoculars of state troopers, above Montgomery and together, holding hands, beneath the white dome's flapping red rag. The blessing—"Hallelujah" and in a low breath—the big, strong Negro beside me squeezed my hand on the "Amen."

We were in the bus somehow, the hot, sweating, thirsty bus and the sun was out now, low before us, we were heading west from the city. We had passed the trucks and clots of uniforms and the long, sturdy lines of rifles and helmets. The faces were unsmiling and seemed to be eager to reprimand us if we stepped where we couldn't. But one smiled, one grinned, and kept grinning and on both sides, they were unsmiling.

Dark now...lights...a valley of lights...Birmingham. And after Birmingham, sleep and bouncing and sleep. St. Louis and morning, snow again. North and the afternoon grew—a sunny afternoon and all of Illinois was on the highway.

What did it mean now? What did we do? The Negro woman sat on her porch in her flower dress. Yeah, we did something. But what does that make me? Back in Valpo, three thousand kids didn't go and I did. I did. I paid down twenty dollars and three days. And they sat at Valpo. So who am I now? But who was I before? And who are they back at Valpo?

A road turned east and U.S. 30 roared us up to Kretzmann's lamp-lit drive and yellow picture window, and in the night behind the house, large and darkly lighted, rose the chapel.

Tremont Murder, Valparaiso March
June 17, 1967

And of course, there had been other marches and there would be more marches.

Like a field of overnight mushrooms, it seemed "marches" were emerging everywhere. This demonstrated a raised public voice against governmental indifference toward issues of human life. They also demonstrated the reluctance of leaders to address instances of injustice. Perhaps the most sobering of these marches for us at LHRAA, came to Valparaiso's doorstep.

It all began about 15 miles to the north—in a little train stop area called Tremont. In a small bar there, a few customers were sipping some refreshment when an African-American steelworker entered, apparently on his return from a hard day's work at the nearby steel mills of Gary. One of the White patrons told him to leave. The Black man claimed his right to stay. His challenger told him he was leaving to get a gun, and if he would still be there when he returned he would shoot him.

The Black man was still there when the angered White man returned; he shot and killed the Black man.

Small articles in the local paper about the jury trial that ensued did not go unnoticed. When readers learned that the jury's verdict declared the accused "not guilty," many were surprised, some shocked, and not a few outraged. Voices of protest were raised especially in the Gary community (about 20 miles to the west of Valparaiso).

Gary's NAACP (National Association for the Advancement of Colored People) announced its plan to bring a busload of people to Valparaiso's County Square—the county seat—to protest what they termed "an open season on Black people."

The city of Valparaiso spent much effort in trying to avoid any kind of response that might prove seriously disruptive. Above the main doors of the courthouse, flags were draped and the balcony was readied for use—public address system and all. The city's Chief of Police was up there keeping an eye on the people gathered below and a rostrum was readied for words from Gary's new mayor, Richard Hatcher, a Valparaiso University Law School graduate, who had just been elected as one of the first Black mayors of major cities in the country.

Word was released that the NAACP of Gary was warned by some more racist-minded folk, that anybody chartering a bus and coming to march on this occasion would go "back to Gary in a casket."

A few of the local White citizenry who insisted on affirming the right of people "to assemble peacefully in redress of grievance" were gathered at the Pennsy railroad station three blocks away from the center of town. They were there to meet the Gary people as they stepped from their bus to walk at their side in a rather small procession to the Porter Country courthouse lawn for the public gathering.

Onlookers huddled in the doorways of stores, nervously watching what was happening. We were walking by twos on the sidewalk and upon our arrival at the place the speakers were gathered, Mayor Hatcher spoke eloquent words alluding to the responsibility of people to conduct their role as citizens responsibly. I was surprised and pleased that one of the marchers stepped up to be my partner in the walk, my young friend, Jody Kretzmann. The threats and fears of violence had subsided, and people were learning to stand up and say what was on their hearts and to practice mutual respect.

And, as at many college and university campuses in those months, there were other expressions of commitment to the cause of justice and peace. On another occasion, when a plaque honoring military heroes was being dedicated and raised—again at the courthouse lawn —a large percentage of Valpo's student body was joined by faculty and some of the administrators of the University. They marched up Lincolnway (the main street) demonstrating their unwillingness to support the continuation of the Vietnam military fiasco.

I remember asking the Dean of Students, somewhat teasingly, "Dean Rubke, are you here to protest the war, or to monitor the behavior of students, or to watch for their safety in this emotional moment?"

He paused for just a second and then thoughtfully said, "Yes, all of them."

CHAPTER 19

NEW ALLIES IN THE SOUTH

L eslie Frerking was the pastor of Ascension Lutheran Church in Charlotte, North Carolina. He would visit people in their homes—did good pastoring. He was a good teacher of the Scriptures.

Two of the people in his study group were Robert and Caroline Miller. Bob and his father were highly recognized as superb orthopedic surgeons. Bob's father had worked with him for many years before his own retirement. But the reputation of the Miller Clinic was well established not only in Charlotte but in surrounding communities as well. Caroline, was a bright woman, an informed and knowledgeable student and also a member of Charlotte's Symphony Orchestra. (I was present for a concert which featured her performing the familiar piccolo obbligato of Sousa's *Stars and Stripes Forever!*)

Doctor Frerking's class at church had been studying the book of Romans, and the Millers raised thoughtful questions about such passages as "Welcome one another as Christ has welcomed us," and "The good that I would wish to do I fail to find myself doing." They asked, "How can the practices of White congregations justify an exclusion of Blacks from their midst?"

Pastor Frerking had come to know the name and the message of Andrew Schulze. This moment called for bringing the Millers to Valparaiso where, at an annual

Institute, they found a warm group of new friends. They refused to justify the segregated South in its tenacious embrace of the Jim Crow attitudes and practice. Their subsequent commitment to support the ministry and teachings of LHRAA was quickly apparent.

Shortly after their return to Charlotte, Caroline called us, asking for information on how to go about sending a railroad car of grain to a starving area in India. Next, we learned that Bob was a leader in getting Charlotte's hospitals to uproot segregated practice towards African-American patients.

Dr. Robert Miller and Nurse Bernice Fulsom, first Black nurse in Charlotte Hospital.

On one occasion, Birmingham's White Pastor Joseph Ellwanger and Black Pastor Will Herzfeld of Tuscaloosa were in the Millers' home in Charlotte. Joe, Will, and I were making a brief "stopover" with the Millers on our way to a pastoral conference where all five of us were to address in Pensacola the next day. Bob thought it wise that we have dinner before catching our flight in late afternoon. I was with him in his study when he phoned one of Charlotte's finest restaurants to make reservations for us. When he told the restaurant manager that one of our group was a dignitary "of color," the answer, Bob told me later: "No problem, Dr. Miller, we'll have a special room for all of you, assuring you of privacy."

"Oh no." Bob answered, "That would make our guest feel conspicuous. If we can't be served among the other tables, we'll simply go to another restaurant."

The restaurant, reluctant to lose a prominent client, changed its policy. I hadn't realized desegregation could be so easy!

Each of the Millers—Bob as well as Caroline—at different times served a term as a member of LHRAA's Board of Directors. They both became speakers at human relations conferences in different parts of the country and wrote articles for LHRAA's monthly *VANGUARD*. Caroline also presented an address to an LHRAA Institute audience.

The Millers were blessed with a bunch of kids—six of them! When they'd drive up from North Carolina for an Institute at Valpo, they'd bring their young ones along. And the Lutze boys would look forward to their coming. highlight of the year!

In the summers, the Millers would usually rent rooms at an ocean-side setting at Myrtle Beach. Caroline's household managing and parental responsibilities, coupled with Bob's professional pressures, necessitated both a change of pace and change of scenery. Their frequent invitations to us to be with them was a sign that they were sensitive to the demands of our dizzying calendar.

Coming to their home was an experience in itself. The white building, located on a winding road graced by ancient trees, as well as carefully pruned and flowering gardens, was three stories tall. Entering the widespread veranda, one found a large living room at the foot of a long, graceful, flowing stairway. There was ample room for dining in the room behind the large fireplace and adjacent to a kitchen with a long table for family eating. And spread around above, on the second floor, were sufficient bedrooms, each with a private bath.

Obviously, here was wealth. And much laughter. And much love. And, of course Ethel, who had entered the family years earlier as a Black housekeeper, was a virtual member of the family.

Ethel was regarded kindly by the neighbors, but her presence was somewhat resented in that the Millers would increase her wages from time to time when the neighbors had no plan to do the same for their African-American household help. But the Millers had seen her stand close by when the children were born, and, as they were growing, needed attention not only for their runny noses, but also for their struggles growing up.

These next lines are hard for me to write. There are few families, in my family's experience, whom we have loved so deeply. It was a Saturday morning that our phone rang. It was Caroline. She was crying and then she said "It's David, our baby. A week ago, we were at a family retreat center and he was climbing around the second-story window frame, slipped and fell to the ground below, not on the driveway, but on a green patch of grass. He was okay, and we came home.

"And then this morning—as usually happens on Saturdays—the kids came into our bedroom and were bouncing up and down. And David slipped and maybe recalling his fall of a week ago, stiffened, and went over the side of the bed, full weight on his head. And he's not going to make it, Karl."

By this time I was bawling and could not say more than, "Oh, Caroline, what can I do?"

She said, "You can come right into our kitchen door this morning and be here with us right now." And somewhat helplessly, I responded, "Oh, I wish I could. I wish I could!"

My wife Esther was standing there next to me and when the conversation ended, we were both crying. Esther finally said, "You know if this were a week from now...." She didn't finish her sentence.

I had been scheduled to go to Alabama to meet with Southern District President, Ed Homrighausen, who felt that LHRAA, and its desegregation work, was making it difficult for pastors in the South. I decided to call him at once and was able to reach him at his office. He remembered that I had planned to be with him Monday afternoon of next week and I asked "Would you be able to have this meeting this coming Monday?" And he responded, "That would be fine."

Phone calls to our travel agents were helpful and they had tickets waiting for me to go to Birmingham via Charlotte, leaving in three hours. Esther drove me to O'Hare Airport and by one o'clock, I was in Charlotte, walking through the Miller's kitchen door.

Close doctor friends had told Caroline, "He simply is not going to make it." She had been to the hospital; Bob asked if I would accompany him to see his child now. Pastor Frerking was out of town, so I was doubly glad that I could be there as pastor and friend. We got to the hospital and went to the room where the littlest Miller, David, lay.

There were four nurses attending him. Bob greeted them all, then he reached out his hand and all of us formed a circle around the little child. Bob said a beautiful prayer; all the nurses were weeping.

We returned to the house and Caroline told me that she had called and made arrangements with the Cannon family, who lived across the street, to bring the children over and use their pool. When we got there, they all quietly slipped into the pool. They said very little to each other and hardly noticed that Ethel had come down, drawn me to the side, whispering "Mrs. Miller asked me to tell you that little David is dying and would you tell each of the children?"

One at a time from the eldest to the youngest, I spoke the news to them. Each responded in sobering comments and chose to be alone, trying to grasp what was happening.

Within an hour or so, the front of the Miller home was crowded with doctors and their wives who had gathered to share the deep feelings they had for their colleague and his family.

That evening, Bob and I went to the airport to meet Lee, the oldest daughter of the six children. She and a few others from her high school class had been in Europe on an exchange program.

While there was joviality on the part of other parents welcoming their children's return, there would be no cheery welcome for Lee's return. She was in near shock when we told her but she insisted on seeing her little brother.

The next morning, I accompanied Bob to the cemetery where we found a family gravesite and returned home. We had several hours to contemplate our past hours and David's brief stay among us.

The day after, I was ready to leave as Pastor Frerking arrived, prepared to assume his role as pastor.

Years passed. The next generation of Millers scattered and/or married. The Miller Clinic expanded, adding new young colleagues to its staff. Bob was doing fewer major surgery assignments and did more "expert witness" tasks in court cases. Health subsided, vitality diminished.

More and more, their care for people in need was focused locally. Caroline became a chef in a soup kitchen, where she served up delicious menus of her own design composed of "day-old" products of local markets. Bob would check in at the Krispy Kreme Donuts shop and fill the back end of his station wagon with donuts for the soup kitchen. And they both had kind words for the guests.

Loving people, precious friends, warming memories —God's gift to us and to countless others. And we heed the Psalmist's word "And forget not all His benefits."

CHAPTER 20
INTERRUPTION:
A WORD TO THE READER

In the first lines of this book, I promised that I intended to share my life journey in the steps of my post-Oklahoma days. I found, however, that certain situations, experiences, and people come to mind in such reflections. These anecdotes and moments of recall are a part of shaping and guiding me in my ministerings. If the reader has read my book "Awakening to Equality," you will also find some of this history recorded there.

I n 1950, when I was still pastor of Hope Lutheran Church in Muskogee, OK, I was requested to check out the possibility for offering a ministry of the Lutheran church to the people of North Tulsa, 60 miles away. Census figures revealed that the population of North Tulsa was comprised almost entirely of Black people. The probing was begun quite independently and primarily by five pastors and a few laymen in Tulsa. The project itself was to be sponsored and supported by the Oklahoma District of the LCMS.

My position in Muskogee was formally called Missionary-at-large of the Oklahoma District, since Hope

Church was not an independent, officially organized congregation of the Oklahoma District.

The proposed venture called for more than these few Tulsa people were able to pursue, so the District officers asked me to explore possibilities. My task then was to prepare a path of procedure. This is the path I developed.

- Step 1: Justify the locating and beginning a new church. True, no resident of North Tulsa had extended an invitation for us to come. What was our motivation?

- Step 2: Find funds to support interns or field workers from the seminaries to assist me and to cover expenses of my continuing to serve Hope Church while spending at least two days in Tulsa each week, exploring the viability of proceeding with such a project.

- Step 3: Determine how the all Black leaders and residents in the larger North Tulsa community and especially the people whose properties would be immediately near the proposed site, would view our purchasing of property and erecting a worship structure.

The District's Board of Directors endorsed the procedure and the program got underway.

In accepting the role, I resisted the idea of my becoming a mere money-raiser to support a new church. Instead, I offered my willingness to visit all 60 Oklahoma LCMS congregations to discuss with them the need to address the White superiority that marked the patterns of life of White people which in reality was contrary to the inclusive spirit and style of Jesus Christ.

If I were to do this, I would invite each of the congregations I'd address to send a contribution to help Oklahoma Lutherans become actively involved in opening the doors to all. The delegates at the District Convention in the following month voted its support for the idea. That launched a heavy schedule of traveling for me to these churches all over the state, and the $4,000+ raised enabled the District to purchase a generous corner lot, ideal for the purposes we had in mind. It was located in the center of a newly developing African-American residential neighborhood, a block away from a city bus stop.

Although there were probably more than three dozen churches in North Tulsa, we counted only three within six blocks of the site we sought, which was located only three blocks from the very, very new Booker T. Washington High School.

Before purchasing any property, I visited with all homeowners adjacent or close to the proposed site, asking whether they would be willing to accept such a new building on the vacant lot that for years had been unattended and unattractive. These people were gracious and even encouraging, so long as whatever structure would be erected there would enhance the attractiveness of the neighborhood.

In those same weeks, I visited with many of the North Tulsa community leaders, soliciting their endorsement of our program. Such a move prudently recognized Tulsa's history of race relations.

In 1921, Tulsa had become the site of a vicious racial explosion.

One leader remembered, "They stopped counting the dead at 100." Attorney B. Franklin informed me he had seen it all, "hiding in a concrete culvert from which point I was able to observe the huge Mack trucks grind their way to dump bodies of the dead in the river."

By the time I arrived in Tulsa in 1952, Tulsans were reluctant to talk about the tragedy. The African-American neighborhood became the center of life for its own Black citizens, making itself a community of its own. There were three pharmacies, one motion picture theater, three accountants, a half dozen groceries, a Negro press (the *Oklahoma Eagle*), three morticians, eating establishments, several small businesses, and of course, several elementary schools, two junior high schools, as well as Booker T. Washington High School.

The community leaders were all wary as I met with them, one by one, explaining our intentions. In general their response was of one voice: "If you come here to add to our community's well-being rather than diminish our values and our independence, we could welcome such partnership." Pastors Stalnaker of the largest Baptist church in North Tulsa and Ben Hill of the Vernon African Methodist Episcopal Church voiced the same sentiment, as did some of the community's attorneys.

We were on our way! One of the top Tulsa architects was intrigued by what we were doing and enthusiastically offered his participation and even agreed to an arrangement where all the craftsmen—electricians, plumbers, masons, carpenters, and others were to be Black, even though they were not eligible for membership in local unions.

Pastor Ben Hill, who also wrote editorials for the *Oklahoma Eagle*, (and later became my very good friend) spoke at the ground-breaking ceremonies (which by the way both neighbors and community leaders attended and to which Carrie Pearson Neeley, Director of Choral Music at Booker T. Washington High School, brought an octet of students from her school to sing for the occasion.)

Everything was on track. The District allocated money to underwrite the program. On paper, arrangements were intact for my returning to Hope Church in Muskogee. A call was issued to Alfred Scholz, graduating from Concordia Seminary in St. Louis, to become the new pastor of Tulsa's Lutheran Church of the Prince of Peace. District Board members were really concerned that after all its investment in the project, there was no assurance of the pastor-elect's capabilities for setting up a new minis-

try. So it was decided to name him as pastor at Muskogee's Hope Church, and move me to Tulsa,
appointing me full-time pastor and developer of the
ministry of Prince of Peace.

My wife, Esther, our boys and I were the congregation's only members.

While the new building was still undergoing construction, the district
dispatched a collapsible
"chapel on wheels" to
the site. This served as
a temporary gathering
place for children in the
neighborhood, whose
parents welcomed our
providing recreation,
singing, crafts, and
story programs for their

Esther, the Lutze boys, and other
Sunday School children..

children in the period between the children's release from
school and the return of parents from their places of
employment.

I found myself visiting homes in the neighborhood,
not so much inviting people to the church as much as
interpreting who we Lutherans were. I wanted to find and
develop ways of sharing with them opportunities to
discover and cultivate enriched meaning for their own,
their families' and their communities' lives.

Simply put, we wanted to help others to center their
lives in Jesus Christ, drawing from His model devoting

conscious loyalty to Him and regarding others as the neighbor to be loved. It was our determined hope that this would be the gift that Prince of Peace's ministry would be to the people of North Tulsa. In all my seven years as pastor there, I was committed to never ask anyone to join our church—to become a Lutheran. Those who wanted to be a part of this community of caring would themselves ask, "What must I do to belong?" And ours became the "growingest" congregation in the District.

The first to become a part of the new congregation were Mrs. Madden, Mrs. Billingslea, Mr. Raymond Jackson and his wife Ruby and his mother, Mrs. Dudley. And loyal they were. They eagerly supplied me with names and addresses of friends who invited me to their homes for visits.

Mrs. Madden asked me to visit a cousin who lived alone with her mother who was in her late eighties. It was a lovely brick house comfortably furnished. The daughter's welcome was gracious. She led me into her living room, where a pitcher of iced lemonade and two glasses awaited us.

Mrs. Madden had told her about Prince of Peace. Her cousin was eager now to hear the whole story of our church. Her interest was genuine. However, as I continued, I felt I was losing the attention of my hostess. She seemed to be making furtive glances at a doorway behind the sofa on which I was sitting. I didn't want to turn away from the good lady, but she seemed to be increasingly disturbed, and she suddenly disrupted my words, shouting, "Mama, you put that gun down right now! This White man is a preacher and he's not come to hurt us or anyone else!"

By then I had turned around and got to see the frail little woman lower the rifle she'd been aiming at the back of my head. I don't recall what happened after that, but the momentary turbulence subsided and I was able to resume my presentation, this time including the calmed grandmother in my audience.

On another occasion—this time at near-midnight—a phone call from Mrs. Madden awakened me, pleading with me to join her at once at Moton Hospital, where another relative, her niece, lay dying. I hurried to the waiting room where Mrs. Madden was seated and weeping, eager to explain to me what had been happening.

The young woman had been dating a boyfriend for well over a year. She had found him mean and abusive and informed him of her decision to discontinue the relationship. On that very night, she accepted a date with a different young man. After their evening together this new suitor had driven her to her home and she approached the door to unlock it. Her jealous former boyfriend stepped from behind a shrub and splashed a bucket of gasoline on her and set her afire.

Now, at the hospital, as we looked at the young woman and saw her covered, literally from head to foot, with a charred crust, the attending emergency physician told us he'd never before seen such an intensive and extensive burn. He made it altogether clear that she would not and could not survive even till morning.

And the doctor left the room.

The patient was heavily sedated, but nonetheless cogent. Mrs. Madden introduced me to her and she immediately responded by telling me she belonged to no church, had never been baptized, and that she wanted so very much to be baptized before taking her last breath.

I spoke as helpfully as possible about our Lord, our faith, and the holy covenant of baptism and the grace our welcoming Lord extends to the people of God. And then I asked for a bowl of water with a towel, and stepped close to the patient's bed. The site was sobering.

No courses at the Seminary ever anticipated this situation. No part of this person's scorched body—hands, legs, face, ears—had been spared by the flames. Where does the water touch the would-be disciple? Well, of course, the bottom of the feet, where the fire had not reached. And the words of our Savior sound clearly: "If I have washed your feet, ought you not to wash one another's feet?"

CHAPTER 21
ROMAN CATHOLICS—
AFFIRMATIVE ACTION AND LOS ANGELES
CHURCH HEAD

espite the fact that the need for dealing with racial problems was screaming for attention, the issues became more and more unattended—surely under-attended. Because the administrators of these churches had so many other problems they were encountering, the social problems facing them called for special and creative programs. For instance, Roman Catholics, in responding to the issue of interracial bias, encouraged the National Catholic Conference for Interracial Justice to take on the matter. Result: a program developed by this commission under the leadership of Mr. Thomas Gibbons and named *Project Equality* seemed especially promising. I had never met Mr. Gibbons before; however, he called me, ostensibly to invite Lutheran participation in the program.

This program was designed to list all commercial enterprises whose CEO and/or Board of Directors were themselves Roman Catholic. Rather than negatively citing firms that were not hiring Black personnel, Project Equality purposely sought out firms that did not exclude Black employees, to support them in their fair policies.

Mr. Gibbons described the program's trial run in St. Louis by way of explaining and illustrating both its project and its effectiveness. As he explained to me, one particular firm for years had been supplying oil to all the Roman Catholic institutions in the St. Louis area. For years now, this firm had received all the orders for oil used in heating all the churches, parochial schools, hospitals, universities, and other church-related units in the diocese.

The Bishop's office inquired whether there had been open bids for this contract. The CEO responded that they had been dealing with each other for years and no other firm had as many tank trucks and other equipment to deliver the needed fuel. Thus, he said, if another firm did want to participate in the negotiating sessions, it might not be able to provide the services needed. He scoffed at the very idea that the church should dictate to any of its members how to conduct a company's sales style.

The church's response: quality of the product or service, the provider's capacity to deliver the product, and the price tagged on the transaction are indeed businesses' legitimate concern. However, the church as a participant in the negotiation, also has the responsibility to be concerned with the moral aspect of the transaction. To be spending such a vast amount of money and not be concerned about fair employment opportunities for people, who are excluded from the work force because of the pigment of their skin, is to compromise moral responsibility.

At the next summer's meeting, the CEO stated he didn't need the church to tell him how to run his business. He would not promise to use preferential treatment to Black workers seeking employment. Apparently he did not intend to employ any personnel who were not White. The Bishop's office found another company willing to hire Black workers. As a result the former employer had a good many empty trucks parked in his lot. He had learned that the church chose a firm that was able to not only provide good service at a reasonable price, but also practiced fair employment and provided fairness in wages for his workers.

Tom then explained his eagerness to meet with me. For Project Equality to become increasingly effective, he said, the program needed a larger ring of participants. Ideally, there should be available a catalog listing firms or organizations that would employ personnel of any racial background in any metropolitan area or small town in the country. Any who choose to be included were required only to apply.

Tom's question: Would I be willing to enlist Lutheran institutions and organizations in the program? It wasn't an everyday occurrence that such overtures of collaboration came to us Lutherans from the Roman Catholic corners.

My answer: Of course. In only a few weeks, statements of endorsement came from all major Lutheran Church body offices and were applauded.

And he had one more request: Would I be his guest and accompany him on a visit to Los Angeles? I would be a resource and support to him, as he would endeavor in his presentation, to persuade the archbishop to install the program in his diocese. My answer again, "Of course."

Tom's presentation, though lucid and persuasive, did not win the day. But in Tom, I'd discovered a new friend and I'd had a rich experience.

CHAPTER 22

LUTHERANS IN AMERICA AND RACISM

In the early years of our country, race relations were not a topic of concern for most of the scattered Lutherans in America. The new settlements spread all over the countryside were more immediately concerned with the support they were giving to new arrivals from European countries. Cities in widespread areas chose names like New London, Germantown, and Berlin in Wisconsin; Paris, Illinois; Holland, Michigan; and New Germany, Minnesota. These choices indicated the intention of these early founders to celebrate and reproduce the culture that was dear to them.

Attending to their own survival and development, these White immigrants were hardly ready to become involved in the issue of slavery and its attending abuse of its victims and their children. And even though the all-White congregations for the most part fervently embraced an uncompromising submission to the Bible, they seemed indifferent to its message that they were to welcome "the stranger within thy gates."

People of color were rarely included in these ethnic communities and already, back in the 1860s, these Black communities had lost young men of their own in the Civil War, in which the flagrant inhumanities inflicted on

Blacks in America were clearly and decisively exposed. Civil Was historians estimate that over 200,000 Black soldiers served in the Civil War and approximately 40,000 died during the war.

However, Lutherans did take very seriously the Scriptural mandate, "Go! Preach the Gospel!" While acknowledging the differences between their own history and cultural heritage and that of the Black neighbors (who in great numbers had been migrating into their vicinities), they regarded these people of color as "mission prospects."

By the time my days of ministry began (in 1945), the number of Black Lutherans in the USA was estimated to be more than 132,000. And the Lutheran church communities proudly claimed these people as Lutheran—almost as trophies in their missionary efforts. Actually, the style and structure of the Lutheran church bodies' relating to these brothers and sisters resembled that of America's South: secular structures where the phrase "separate but equal" had gained such widespread acceptance.(And not always so equal. . .)

The White Church eagerly reached out to embrace these members of God's family—but at arm's length! Schools at Selma, Alabama and Greensboro, North Carolina, supported largely by the LCMS Conference, played a strong role in becoming focal points for diagnosing the situation that impeded and in many instances prevented the genuine bonding of White Lutherans with their neighbors of color. And those who supported continuance of this educational structure were really saying, "It's good enough for Negroes." While Greensboro included seminary training at its campus, Selma had a grade school, high school, and college on its campus.

A significant majority of African-American Lutheran church workers were graduates of these institutions. The curricula these schools offered were far less demanding than those provided at the two all-White seminaries and eleven preparatory schools of the LCMS. Decision-making in the organization (as well as true mutual involvement in God's mission) inevitably was flawed by that overarching style of paternalism that marked the relationship.

One can almost imagine defenders of such an arrangement pointing out the weaknesses in education offerings in the public elementary schools of the time, especially in the South. In essence, they were justifying the system saying, "We give the students we teach at Greensboro and Selma courses they can intellectually handle and that will prepare them to serve adequately simple folk of the cotton fields who don't require deep intellectual shepherding." Graduates of that system were eligible for ordination and service in General Conference (Negro) churches, but not in LCMS churches.

LHRAA was actively involved in efforts to close down both the Selma and Greensboro schools. Admittedly, some students benefitted from these institutions through the years. As the saying goes: "Something beats nothing." However, in all the years that passed, there were no indications of any of Missouri Synod's schools developing recruiting programs to enroll Black Lutheran students. When questioned about this, some of administrators of the all-White schools explained that they did not want to make it more difficult for Greensboro and Selma to recruit Black students.

By 1945, three of these previously all-White schools had each enrolled one student, who, by the way, were all ordained and subsequently served in Missouri Synod congregations—Pastors Jeff Johnson, Albert Pero, and Samuel Hoard.

The decision was made by the church leaders to close Immanuel Greensboro and to concentrate all their resources to improve the quality of the Selma school.

PART II:

FAMILY AND FRIENDS ARE ALLIES

CHAPTER I
FAMILY TOGETHER

I have certainly traveled a large number of miles through the years. However, I had never gotten around to totaling the distance covered or the time spent away from home. And many of my away-from-home days were richly rewarding, stacked high with new and often exciting experiences.

I did, however, treasure times I could be with my family.

That's why mealtime was so important. Esther consistently pampered us with delicious food. And the four boys' teasing and joshing were no less important—nor the stories about what happened in our lives since the last time we sat together. And these sessions were occasion for me to acknowledge their role in caring for and helping their mother in times of my absence. They were participants in my ministry. It was as exciting for them as it had been for me when I had my experience with the FBI in Phoenix.

I had flown to Phoenix to meet with some of the members of the American Indian Movement (AIM), a group self-described as a militant organization of Native Americans determined to awaken our nation to its past dishonorable relations and malpractice towards the original Americans). I had no sooner checked in and opened the door to my motel room when my phone rang.

The voice on the line was soft spoken and cordial. He identified himself as an FBI agent and addressed me by name. He told me he was informing me of his knowledge of my coming to Phoenix to meet with two Native American men who had already checked in. His call was intended to warn me that these men (Dennis Banks and Clyde Bellcourt) were known to be dangerous. He advised me not to meet with them, suggesting that I return home.

I'm sure that during the course of the previous three years, I had met with Dennis and Clyde at least a half dozen times or more. I was meeting with these men to help them negotiate with Lutheran Church bodies to develop a program for Native American youth in the Midwest. I told the FBI agent I found federal surveillance of such a meeting most inappropriate.

On a later occasion, Esther, son Mark, and I had made a trip to Colorado with Lynn and Merry (her birthday was on Christmas!) Redding and their kids. At a Nebraska conference, we had seen Clyde and he urged us to go through South Dakota as we traveled on our return trip to Indiana. Lynn was very willing to make the adjustment and confided that when he was very small, he had told his mother he wanted be an Indian when he grew up! He was persuadable now.

When we arrived near dawn at the Red Bud Reservation, our agreed-upon meeting place, we found ourselves in the midst of witnessing a celebration of the Sun Dance. To the steady, plaintive chanting of the singers and the rhythmic pounding of the drum, off to the side a bit stood the Medicine Man, solemnly presiding in this sacred moment, explaining to the wide circle gathered there the significance of the event with deep reverence. Among the crowd of probably 125 or so, the Reddings, Esther, Mark (a teenager then), and I were probably the only White people present.

A tree had been planted in the center of the space designated as the worship center. This obviously symbolized the presence of God. Four gateways were marked off, one for each direction of the compass, each attended by a woman. The ten main figures in the circle began dancing around the tree, blowing whistles they had carved beforehand for this occasion. Dancing with them in their circular pattern were probably a dozen men who were a part of the drama. These all came to seek God's holiness for a new venture or path in their lives. One following the other, they approached the tree and submitted to a leader, who would cut a piece of flesh from the arm of the participant, who then would return to his place among those dancing around the tree. The shedding of blood depicted the painful confrontation for sins of the past.

And then followed the climax of the solemn event. Each of the inner circle whistle-blowing subjects, as a token of commitment and total dependence on the Great Spirit of Life, would lie on the ground before the tree while a holy man would reach up to grasp a strand of sinew fastened twelve feet or so up the pole. Attached to the end of the cord was an eagle claw, which would be inserted deep in the flesh of the man's chest. He was then helped to his feet moving backwards until the inserted claw tore through the flesh, to dangle loosely while the dancer resumed his earlier position and joined the dance with his comrades. It took well over an hour to complete the ceremony. To be there was a sobering experience from which one could not leave without knowing that we'd seen so much more than mere exhibitionism.

And this was especially so, for us, as we saw Clyde Bellcourt step forward and submit to his piercing, first on his left side and then on his right, as he spelled out in this act his desire for God's company as he undertook a commitment to help his people. As with all those who submitted to the piercing, Clyde, the only participant twice pierced, was being fanned by an assistant with a large leafy branch; he slowly rose to his feet and resumed his place, dancing with his partners.

We were deeply moved. And so was Mark.

Some weeks later, a small article appeared in a Minneapolis paper reporting that Clyde Bellcourt had been arrested for a crime. He had stolen a sausage from a supermarket.

In all my years, I have never before or since seen a newspaper article telling of a person stealing a sausage. Those lines tell of a man who was hungry; he was too ashamed to beg and brave enough to have been pierced in commitment to his people's children. I remember the principle of justice calling for punishment to fit the crime, but this punishment was certainly too harsh for this "crime." I tried, but was never able to reach Clyde to show my concern and respect.

Table of Surprises

When son Peter attended VU, he lived only a few blocks from our home. Even so, he was much involved in things on campus. He did check in to see how things were going on the home front, but in many respects, he might as well have been enrolled with his brother Steve, who was a student in faraway Princeton.

Tom, a high school student, was increasingly involved in the excitement of the decade, along with O.P. Kretzman's son, Steve, and Janet Springsteen.

Janet lived next door, resorted to our basement in order to make large placard signs to enlist followers in a "March for Hunger" right here in Valparaiso. By the way, the event attracted far more participants than they had anticipated. After it was over, they returned to our house and we found them sitting around a table with an impressively large pile of bills and coins contributed by supporters of the venture. The young enthusiasts welcomed me because they had found themselves without a clue as to what they should do with all the money that had suddenly come their way. As I remember, I believe I put them in touch with Bread for the World. An annual Hunger March is still observed in our town.

Later, Tom's interest in social concerns was shown in his work in the "Mansion" in Chicago. Being there brought new learning experiences. Tom did an "overnighter" at the Mansion. Having dismounted from a bus, he was making his way down a very dark street near the University of Chicago. It was very late when he noticed a figure coming his way—on the other side of the street. As the man came closer, he passed under light pole that provided enough light for Tom to discern the man was probably twentyish and Black.

No cars passed by and no one else in sight. He was hardly prepared for a confrontation. He only had a few dollars in his wallet. Perhaps the man would be willing to settle for his watch. As he saw the man begin to cross the street towards him, he knew he could not get away. Suddenly the man was in front of him and said "Can you help me? I have to go to visitation at a funeral home and I don't know how to tie this tie."

Tom saw that the man was neatly dressed and had his tie hanging in front of his dress shirt. Tom said "I only know how to do it this way" and he stepped behind the man, and coming around his back, put his arms around this stranger's neck, did his best to make a presentable tie from this position. Stepping back in front of the man, he adjusted the knot and they both stepped back into the night and continued their separate journeys.

Those were the times of an unsettled climate of discontent, marked by protests, and disruptions in the cities, and turmoil on the country's campuses, armed military presence, assassinations and a hopeless and botched commitment of our troops in Viet Nam—all combined to evoke responses of anger, confusion, and frustration. There was little escape from the widespread and often wild-spread uneasiness that surfaced in so many gatherings these days.

The growing independence and activism of the four Lutze sons became increasingly noticeable—as a result, there were fewer and fewer times of bringing us all together at mealtime. This, in turn, provided fifteen-year old Mark with more opportunity to speak up and be heard. His message—simple, brief, firm, to the point: "I'm going to Washington on Thursday to be in the May Day event, a demonstration of college students from all over the country protesting US involvement in Viet Nam, and some VU students are driving there, so I've got a ride."

His mother immediately responded. Her message? Simple, brief, firm, to the point: "Oh, no you don't!"

Anticipating his mother's opposition to his planned venture, Mark had been storing away coins "for such a time as this." Aside from the cost factor, he was armed with a rather complete arsenal of ready answers for any rationale his mother might propose to frustrate his determined intentions.

I offered a compromise position to solve the standoff. "Let's call Steve up at Princeton and ask him to meet you in Washington. He would be a bit more versed in this kind of experience."

When I had been in New York, Steve came into the city to have dinner with me and as we walked past a somewhat unimpressive hotel, he was prompted to say, "Dad, this is a hotel you ought to stay in when you are in New York. When we were part of the demonstration in this area and police had dispersed us with tear gas, this hotel was handing out wet washcloths to those of us who had been sprayed. They're good people."

When I replied, "You never even told us about your being in on this," he excused himself saying "We didn't have much time for writing letters!"

When we called Steve, his first response was his informing us that on the previous weekend he and some of his Princeton friends had already been in D.C. for a "practice drill." Nonetheless, he said, he'd not been spending much time with his youngest brother in the past two years and he agreed to serve as his chaperone for a weekend.

Elmer Witt's daughter Anne had an apartment in Washington and agreed to provide sleeping accommodations for them. Mark's mother agreed. Mark agreed. All the road blocks removed.

Upon their arrival in Washington, our sons headed for the agreed-upon gathering site. A bus stopped where they were, and police in trench coats left the bus and— determined to nip in the bud the very beginning of any disruptive demonstration—swooped down and took aside any pedestrians of college age on the streets. The Lutze boys were separated from each other. Steve was arrested and hustled off to a court scene, where he paid his fine and was released and left to search for his kid brother, wherever he might be.

Down the hall from Anne's apartment, a friendly D.C. policeman tried to be helpful in their search. Steve felt awful. He called us and told us they had become separated and he was looking for Mark.

Meanwhile, back in Valparaiso, we stayed awake into the past-midnight hours, helpless. Finally, the phone rang. The woman calling identified herself as a social worker. She told us she had Mark at her side. He was safe and well. She told how he, with hundreds of others, had been herded into a huge stadium and had now been released. She continued, "He is very, very tired, and a bit disoriented and very much in need of sleep."

Then she handed her phone to Mark, who indeed sounded very tired, but assured us of his good health.

The widespread turmoil of this period of a country in distress spilled into our family life, too. The boys were safe, their mother calmed, but I realized that the choices I had been making were closely observed by my sons and their activism was both cause for concern and affirmation.

We would often, at dinnertime, talk about the invitation of our Lord, "Follow Me."

And in our bedtime prayers, we gave thanks for our sons' safety. We felt the Lord must be pleased with all of them.

CHAPTER 2
MY FRIEND ELMER

W ay back in my prep school days in Milwaukee, I got to know this skinny, little kid who wore glasses, who seemed to show up in a hundred places, and was always sparkling with fun. I was sixteen and he was two years younger. We both sang in the school's Glee Club, which would tour Wisconsin and nearby states, singing concerts in churches, doing public relations work for the school, generating support, and recruiting new students. That's probably when I got best acquainted with Elmer. And though neither of us could even turn a somersault, let alone cartwheels and other gymnastic twists, we must have been recognized for strong lungs and hefty vocal cords and were invited to join the truly agile and acrobatic classmates of mine, Gottfried "Jeep" Press and Luther Schwartzkopf, on the all-boys' school's cheerleading squad.

On weekends at our boarding school, many of the dormitory rooms were emptied as students, whose homes were not too far distant from our campus, left to be with their families. After registering with the President's Office, students could apply for permission to move in with friends whose roommates' beds had been vacated for the weekend.

On one particular weekend, Elmer's Aunt Lil had come to our campus to take him home to Forest Park

(Illinois) to spend a weekend with his family. I accepted her invitation to come along. That's when I got to know the members of the Witt family: oldest brother, Vernon, worked for the American Can Company and sang in a Chicago male chorus; Ernie, a lineman for Illinois Bell; Carl, still in elementary school, and later a teacher. And, of course, there was their mother, Anne. She was a warm, loving, patient woman, who often was made the brunt of family jokes. The entire group would be best described as possessing a tireless, raucous sense of humor.

During all my time with the family that weekend, I had not yet met Mr. Witt. After the Sunday morning service at St. John Lutheran Church, Elmer led me to a small room so that I might meet his father. He, together with four other gentlemen, was seated at a round table stacked high with the contribution envelopes and other offerings gathered in the morning's worship service. Elmer moved close and spoke to his father: "Dad, this is my friend Karl, who came home with me this weekend."

Not even looking up from the mound of coins heaped before him, his dad responded, "Can't you see I'm counting money?" Then spreading some of the coins before him, he began to sort them into two piles. As if speaking to himself, he continued, "Two for me, two for the church; two for me, two for the church," until all the men in the room burst out laughing. And I quickly realized who the centerpiece of this family's hilarity was.

Some time later—it was again a weekend on which a good number of students had left the campus to be with their families back home—and all my five roommates had checked out, and Elmer's had also left for the two days. He registered with the President's Office to spend the weekend in my room. At 10:30, residence hall lights were extinguished, serving notice to the students that they should be bedded down. Since the red exit lights at the ends of each corridor shed only the very dimmest illumination, the different professors, taking their turns each evening, used bright flashlights on their rounds to check whether students were in bed for the night.

Elmer and I were deep into sleep that Friday night when I was awakened by a hand on my shoulder and the blinding beam of a flash light. The man's voice whispered, "Lutze! Lutze, wake up." I realized it was Dr. Rincker, the school's president. "Is that Elmer Witt in the bed over there?"

When I assured him it was, he told me Elmer's dad was near death. He had come to wake Elmer and to break the news to him. I was to get up, help him dress, pack, and prepare him for going home. Dr. Rincker had already checked timetables and promised to return in two hours to take Elmer to the depot to catch the North Shore train for Chicago. Until then, I was to stay with him and be prepared to ride along to the station.

Then he woke Elmer to share the word about his father and let us know he would return for us later. And I was to be there to keep Elmer company. Together, we sat on the side of his bed, trying to put together all that our unexpected night visitor had told us. I had a little pocket flashlight and we went to Elmer's room to gather things he would take with him.

We left his bag inside the door of the dorm and went into the night for a walk. The school was located in a quiet residential neighborhood. No people in sight. The windows of the houses were all dark. We were quite by ourselves. Two little guys walking nowhere. And talking. And talking.

Talking about families, death and funerals. And our own, too. Talking about God. After all, sometime in the distant future—very distant—we would be pastors. We talked about nights and mornings. About friendships. We had never had a conversation like this. It was serious. It was deep. And it was late. And as we returned to the dormitory, the President arrived to take us to the train station.

A few days later, President Rincker took me along on his trip to Illinois to attend Mr. Witt's funeral. I sat with the family. I hadn't begun to realize that an unimaginably strong, enduring bonding had occurred between Elmer and me. Years later—I was serving as pastor in Oklahoma by then—I was totally surprised when Elmer phoned, asking me to perform his marriage to Ginny.

In later times when we'd be together, I'd often mention to others that I had indeed performed their marriage and invariably with a straight face, Elmer would quickly add, "Oh, yes! I'll never forget that sermon based on the Scripture account of the woman taken in the act of adultery!" For a brief moment listeners would be slightly stunned until they realized they'd been taken! He never did lose his quick humor. And anyone could understand why the family name was Witt.

The close interwovenness of the Lutzes and the Witts also found expression in intimate family moments. Elmer spoke the homily at the funeral services of my father and my mother. Both of us participated in each of our two marriage celebrations.

* * * * *

Elmer's Career Unfolds

I don't know how many others Elmer phoned on the day he was informed that his first post as a young pastor would be in California. By that time, I was deeply ensconced in my ministry in Oklahoma. I vividly remember his excitement as he shared with me the details of his new assignment.

He was to serve as pastor to a three-site parish—small congregations—in Barstow, Needles, and Victorville near the Mojave Desert, in California. Anyone choosing to rank congregations would probably quickly dismiss this trio as less-than-prestigious—or noteworthy. Yet in a short paragraph in the official paper

Elmer Witt.

of the national church body, a columnist did indeed mention this as probably the most spread-out Lutheran parish in the country, where, in circuit-rider style, the pastor would travel 253 miles every Sunday to conduct services at each of the three churches.

Elmer and I both found ourselves busy in our work. However, we did manage regularly to update each other on what we were doing. In my case, I had found myself volunteering as part-time (un-salaried, of course) director of a youth camp (named Lutherhoma) during the summer. Meanwhile, Elmer became involved with programs of the Southern California District Walther League. At that time, the Walther League had become an officially recognized—but independent—national youth organization of the LCMS.

The Walther League Days

The League was clearly serving as a wholesome Christian alternative for youth to resist the secular world's alluring lifestyle, which seemed to be encroaching on small parochial communities everywhere.

In its earlier days, the Walther League found its membership largely among people of late or post-high school age. The League and its programs provided social opportunities for Lutherans of that age bracket.

Dr. Walter A. Maier, later to become nationally famous as an outstanding radio evangelist, was Executive Secretary of the League in the early 1920s. I recall his comment when asked whether the League had become a sort of Lutheran "match-making" organization. Maier conceded, "It is true that many young men and young women who would attend Walther League functions would find their life mate at these meetings, ultimately become engaged, and marry." He said simply, "Is this a bad thing, even though it isn't the primary aim of the League's program?"

More, however, than only giving young people opportunity to find new friends and share in activities together, Walther League programs pressed for cultivating intellectual and spiritual growth. Since many of the Leaguers, upon leaving high school, would go directly into the work world without benefit of a college experience, they found what the League offered to be a desirable resource for their personal development. With a menu before them of lectures, debates, essays, and study of both historical and contemporary topics, as well as cultural and religious subjects, Leaguers found participation both stimulating and challenging.

By 1934, the membership of the League reached the 50,000 mark. Because many of the Leaguers were employed, they were able to make financial contributions to the League. This made it possible for the League to offer in its programs opportunities for service, as well as for learning.

One such program sought to provide hostel facilities to serve young people leaving rural communities, as they sought a new life in some of the nation's larger cities.

More spectacularly, already back in the twenties, the League also reached out to people assaulted by tuberculosis, establishing first a tent medical center in Wheat Ridge, Colorado, (which later would develop into a full-fledged hospital), where patients could receive the kind of special medical care required for treating that vicious malady. Leaguers were so supportive of this venture that they not only were able to pay off the mortgage and to build a wing to the hospital, but also to contribute to its operational costs.

At that time, many of the church's young people were children or grandchildren of immigrants from Germany. These immigrants, while desiring to be loyal and responsible American citizens, also harbored fond memories and strong love for their old homeland and loved ones they had left behind. Most of the LCMS congregations offered two services each Sunday—one in English and one in German.

Now, in the early 1900s, some of the first- or second-generation offspring of these forebears, though proud to be Americans, were reluctant to find fault with the rise of Hitler in Germany. Drawing on their personal history and cultural roots, they still had fond memories of earlier days in the land that had been the cradle of the Lutheran Reformation. Proud of their religious heritage, they still sang with gusto the hymns that were born, sung, and treasured back in their earlier days in "their fatherland."

The Walther League in its publications was one of the few voices in the LCMS to speak out against the flagrant anti-Semitism that so many tried to justify as a defense against communism. Many church leaders of local congregations registered uneasiness about the way some of the contemporary social issues were being addressed in League publications. More and more of these voices expressed their concern by withdrawing financial support of the League.

* * * * *

When Dr. Andrew Schulze wrote his book, *My Neighbor of Another Color*, it received a scathing review by St. Louis Seminary Professor John Theodore Mueller in the *Lutheran Witness*, the LCMS's official house organ.

Concordia Publishing House had refused to publish the book. However, members of Pastor Schulze's St. Philip Lutheran congregation in St. Louis underwrote the cost of its publication. The book enjoyed only meager marketing support, until the negative review by Mueller appeared. More and more people wanted to examine this book so severely attacked and all copies were sold. Under the leadership of Dr. O.H. Theiss, the Walther League underwrote a second printing, which also sold out.

Schulze in his later book, *Race Against Time*, tells how Dr. Mueller years later, told him how his own attitudes on the issue had changed and expressed his regrets that he had written the piece.

By the time World War II was underway, the League's membership had diminished by half. Once the war was over, the League's health rallied. Between 1940 and 1949, the number of local League societies across the country had grown from 1,239 to 3,307. At the close of 1945, the League's ledgers revealed assets in excess of $75,000 in cash and security reserves. The staff had worked creatively and conscientiously to develop programs of service, such as drawing post-war military personnel into local societies of the League, which provided social activities and dinners in homes and support for young men and women away from home. The League's leaders also introduced a program of direct relief to Europeans devastated by the war.

In 1934, Dr. O.P. Kretzmann, successor to Walter A. Maier, left his position with the Walther League to become President of Valparaiso University in Indiana. Dr. Theiss, who succeeded O.P. Kretzmann, together with his staff, worked on programs to cultivate leadership for youth ministry at local levels.

While I was still pastor in Oklahoma, I was among some forty clergy and teachers Dr. Theiss invited to a Youth Leadership Training Retreat at Druce Lake, Illinois. We, in turn, would be asked to serve as "deans" in week-long Lutheran Service Volunteers (LSV) schools intended to prepare Leaguers across the country for leadership roles in their congregations. That was how I became committed to involvement in the Walther League.

The G.I. Bill made enrollment in college an attractive option for young people who were returning from military service during World War II. A greater number of new members to the League were younger teenagers. That fewer older Leaguers had found employment in earning positions spelled decreasing income for the organization. By 1949, however, attempts to make the League's program richer and more effective proved expensive and the bottom line in its books reflected a $4,999 deficit.

In spite of valiant efforts by the staff, the League had fallen on hard times. Dr. Theiss left his post to become President of a newly formed Lutheran Seminary in Japan. The vacated position was hardly an attractive one. There surely was no long string of candidates lined up to apply for the job he had held for the Walther League.

Who would have thought that in choosing a successor to such well-known leaders as Dr. Maier and Dr. Kretzmann, the search committee would start looking near the Mojave Desert to consider engaging a relatively young preacher who had virtually no experience in organizational and administrative leadership? When Elmer Witt called me to tell me that he had been invited to apply for the position, he was clearly overwhelmed by the invitation. He had never set his eyes—or hopes—on assuming the role required by the League in its proposal to him.

We must have talked for more than an hour, trying to explore all the facets of the position to which he would have to address himself. Because of the close ties that had developed between us through the years of our friendship, (in later years my colleague and mentor, Dr. Andrew Schulze, remarked, "That's the kind of friendship the Scriptures ascribe to the relationship of Jonathan and

David!") I felt I knew Elmer's gifts, his commitment, and his potential better than any search committee. When we came to the end of our conversation, both he and I were convinced that this was a challenge and an opportunity which he could—and should—explore seriously. And I assured him of my support.

Before hanging up the phone (half in jest but only half!), I told him one assignment that I was imposing on him, if he were to accept the post: "Do everything you can to replace the organization's theme song, *Walther Leaguers, Walther Leaguers, One and all are we!*" Its words could hardly be regarded as deathless poetry and its tune would surely not enjoy acclaim at any self-respecting school of music. The old song, however, proved too deeply embedded in the memories and hearts of long-time Leaguers to ever disappear. Later on, however, Elmer did introduce into the League's repertoire the strong hymn, *O God of Youth*, which found its way into the *Lutheran Book of Worship*, a hymnal jointly published by the Fortress Press and Concordia Publishing House.

The League flew the young candidate to Chicago for the interview. Later that evening, I received my call from Elmer reporting on the events of the day. He was obviously excited. All had gone well. Both Elmer and the League personnel obviously were pleased with the meeting and seemed to regard the teaming as a fine fit, auguring well for the League's future and young Witt's ministry.

Once behind the large, beautiful desk in his Chicago office, Elmer found himself in far more frequent conversations with me than either of us had ever anticipated. The League was hardly a faded flower at the time Elmer took office. Surely the League had been effective in its support of Wheat Ridge and the Hostel program and European post-war relief. It had been enlisting local Leagues in raising thousands of dollars for ministries of various kinds in this country and abroad. Its annual national conventions were attracting in the neighborhood of 1,500 young people from all over the country.

Elmer was eager to build on the best of his predecessors' programs and to strengthen the role of the League in the lives of his church's youth. He felt one particular avenue for pursuing that aim lay in enriching the annual national conventions of the League. He had wanted to sharpen the focus for convention participants on both Scripture study and on cultivating an awareness of the potential for effective service to be found in Christians joining together to do what they might never be able to accomplish alone.

Until then, conventions were usually held in some of the larger hotels in the country's metropolitan centers. More and more of the Leaguers who attended were younger and distractions provided by "the Big City" abounded. Elmer and his staff agreed that selecting college or university campuses might be advantageous as sites for these events. Moving from hotel to campus would provide the annual meetings with an atmosphere of a retreat. Participants would be housed in residence halls.

All this prompted a phone call to me from Elmer. I was serving as pastor in Tulsa then. Did I have any ideas about how to identify, enlist, and prepare some mature adults to serve as counselors? Individuals would be enlisted and assigned to groups as discussion leaders and counselors. The ensuing conversation was lengthy, lasting far into the hours of the night.

End result: I accepted his assignment to organize and carry out the program as head counselor at the League's convention to be held at Oklahoma State University in Stillwater in the summer of 1957. Until the time of the event itself, he and I were in phone conversation at least twice a week.

The gathering was counted a success and plans were already underway for the following year's meeting. This one was scheduled for Miami University of Ohio in Oxford, Ohio. When asked, I agreed to take on the post of head counselor once more—but this time I was to have an assistant (whom I had never met before) by the name of Professor Walter Reiner, football coach at Valparaiso University.

But that's another story—just the beginning of a wonderful story, which I will tell later.

* * * * *

1958 would be my final year as pastor in Oklahoma. By the following summer, I would be on my way to Valparaiso to begin my new work there. This called for my declining Elmer's request to participate in the Walther League convention on the campus in Lansing, Michigan.

I was still pastor in Tulsa, however, when Elmer called me to report on another program he and his staff had launched. His office had earlier received messages from a good many pastors seeking help in revitalizing youth programs in their parishes. The League responded by contacting certain clergymen around the country, pastors recognized as already having effective programs of youth ministry in their own parishes. These pastors were asked to nominate names of particularly bright, capable, and responsible youth in their congregations who might be helpful in developing a Caravaning Program. Reviewing the applications of nominees submitted, the League's staff selected 33 finalists.

These young people subsequently participated in a sort of correspondence course in the spring to prepare them for an intensive week together, which would ready them for a summer in which they'd be dispatched in teams of three to different regions of the country. In these sessions of preparation, they would learn ways of leading group Bible study, songs that were fun to sing, ideas on recreation and games, organizational structuring, program planning, and more.

After those days of cramming as much as the Caravaners could possibly grasp into one short, exciting week, they were deemed ready to visit parishes that sought to energize their youth ministries. The Caravaners would be having sessions with pastors and other congregational leaders, with youth, and with parents.

After two sets of three full and very busy days visiting two host congregations—and having fairly well divested themselves of all that they had been prepared to share—these Caravaners were to enjoy a day of respite, move to a new site, and catch their breath before their next three-day stint at another congregation.

Elmer's reading of the first year of the program was enthusiastic. Apparently pastors who had hosted the teams were elated with the experience. The League's staff was ready to do a repeat. The program was to be expanded to enlist 54 Caravaners to compose 18 teams.

There was, however, one issue that repeatedly appeared on the post-event evaluation sheets submitted by staff, site pastors, and by Caravaners themselves. In several instances, tensions had surfaced among members of some of the teams. Several claimed to have experienced exclusion or abandonment or mistreatment. Some faulted teammates for not accepting their share of responsibility. Some lamented a teammate's homesickness; another, a teammate's arrogance. When Elmer listed for me all the items included on the agenda of the week-long preparation course, I suggested that more attention might be given to the concern for human relations, providing help in developing reciprocal respect for—and just plain getting along with—teammates and with all the people Caravaners would encounter during their experiences.

Elmer agreed and asked whether I would join the staff in the following summer's Caravaners' briefing sessions, to lecture and lead discussions on "Getting Along With People." I was also asked to assist in determining which groupings of three might be best suited for working together. Filling that role for the next three summers—my last year in Oklahoma and my first two in Valparaiso—proved to me wonderfully enriching.

Working closely with Walther League staff members Walter Wangerin, Sr., Carl Streufert, Jolan Schwass, Dick Hemma, and Alfred Klausler—together with those beautiful, talented Caravaners—proved an enriching contribution to my life and ministry. I prize those hours together with both the youth and the staff and I treasure those friendships highly.

Some of these Caravaners were in their college years; a few had not yet finished high school. They were an exceptionally bright lot, drawn from a variety of backgrounds: some from rural settings, a good many from suburban communities, a few from large metropolitan centers, a sprinkling from Southwest ranches, some with accents that revealed their deep South roots. Being with them for seven days in all their waking hours, studying them, listening to their stories, capturing their openness, their excitement, and their creativity combined to make this a marvelous learning experience for me. I still maintain ties with many of them. And one especially— Gail Jones (Blask), who would become my wife in 1996.

Elmer and I stayed in touch through the years, The Witts' home, first in Park Forest and later in nearby Matteson, was only an hour away from ours in Valparaiso. Since the five Witt kids—Anne, Barb, Paul, Tom, and Mary—got along well with our four sons—Peter, Steve, Tom, and Mark—and since our wives enjoyed being together, we'd often exchange family visits. This afforded valuable time for Ginny and Esther to share their stories and, not infrequently, to slip off to a nearby AmVets outlet store to pounce upon unbelievably generous bargains for enhancing both families' wardrobes.

Elmer and I would often meet halfway for breakfast sessions together and update each other on what was going on in our work. Elmer was very supportive of my working with churches—as well as with students—in interracial matters. And between such sessions there were ample occasions for us to support each other in ministry. Elmer could be counted on for speaking at different meetings that dealt with race relations—including the annual Valparaiso University Institutes on Human Relations.

The two of us would often be on the phone together. On one such occasion, he was particularly concerned about an impending Walther League convention scheduled for the following summer of 1963, in Washington, D.C. Witt and his staff wanted very much to help the young people who would be attending to become aware of the racial issues that confronted the country at the time, with a view towards facing these from a Christian perspective.

In envisioning program possibilities, Elmer and his staff had they agreed it might be effective to invite a well-known African-American to introduce the subject of race in a keynote presentation. The name that quickly surfaced was Dick Gregory, popular humorist known for his gift of discussing problems in race relations, yet doing so with wry and insightful wit.

Problem: Dick Gregory did most of his performances in night clubs, where he was accustomed to using a vocabulary that seemed hardly appropriate in a situation like this churchly youth gathering. Elmer's request: would I be willing to sit in on a meeting with this celebrity in order to determine whether this idea was feasible—and wise. I agreed to attend.

Meeting Dick Gregory was an experience in itself. He was tired, for he had not been to bed since his most recent performance well after midnight in the day's early hours. While regretting his tardiness, he was not apologizing. There was no attempt to be impressive and he was quite willing to get into the conversation we'd come for without belaboring the niceties and formalities of getting acquainted.

Although I expected to be an advisor at this meeting it soon became clear that my role was to guide this breakfast conversation by interviewing Gregory. I first described the organization to him as one that attempted to take Lutheran Youth out of their parochial corners to learn about the realities of life and in their new awareness to respond constructively in a way consistent with the

Christian faith. I told him that we were convinced that he had the gift of interpreting the issues of race, as well as a commitment to help people to understand, and even become more committed to participate in championing change.

I then explained to him that the audience he'd be addressing would consist largely of White young people between 13 and 23 years of age. Probably most of them would come from the Midwest, and probably most of them would never have met or even spoken with a person of color before in their entire life. Therefore this was to be a valuable and growing experience for them.

When our committee asked whether he would consider taking on the assignment, Gregory seemed to hesitate, wondering whether he could adapt his style to such an audience. After thinking it through, he looked up and said he could envision himself doing this in interview style. Then, pointing at me, he said, "I'll do it if he does it with me." The only props he asked for: two tall bar stools and a microphone to be set up between us with the two of us engaging in dialog.

On the day we were to be "on stage," there was a bit of anxiety on the part of the convention program committee gathered in our Washington hotel room. I had not been in contact with our guest I was to interview. No outline or notes had been prepared. It was only two hours before our guest was scheduled to speak—and the man had not yet arrived!

Suddenly Dick Gregory was at the door.

He looked tired and explained that he didn't feel well —an upset stomach. He had not slept. He asked for the house phone and called room service, requesting that a box of baking soda be sent to our room. The delivery came quickly and he immediately took a spoonful of the white powder in a glass of water.

After only a very short while, he announced that he already felt relief. He began to pontificate: "If someone would simply fatten the price of this stuff and sell it as a miracle medicine, he'd be a millionaire in a year!"

Still holding the phone in one hand, he took a small slip from his wallet and dialed another number. "I want to talk with Robert Kennedy." Raising his voice, he said, "No, I want to talk with Attorney General Robert Kennedy — you tell him, Dick Gregory is calling!"

There was a long pause—all of us in the room were quiet. Then he continued, "Hi, Bobby. I'm going to be speaking to a group now, but I'll give you a call at about five and we can talk about it then. Good-bye."

The Washington Interview

In his opening remarks to the audience of more than 3,000 conventioneers, Gregory spoke of the difference between the people of the North and those of the South. Addressing the issue of civil rights demonstrations, Gregory noted the courageous character of these protests: "Their cause is the call for freedom–for basic human rights."

What possibilities are there for the Church and its members to address these issues? Gregory pointed out that for hundreds of years the White churches have stepped back from seizing opportunities to stand with the Negro.

In the paragraphs that follow, I am including a verbatim transcript of the recording, a telescoped summary of the interview held at the Walther League convention.

Announcer: The open-end discussion on human relations was introduced by the Reverend Karl Lutze, professor of religion at Valparaiso University and Field Secretary for the Lutheran Human Relations Association with Mr. Dick Gregory, a noted entertainer, lecturer, and advocate of human rights. This recording brings you a telescoped summary of the dialogue and the frank discussion by youth that followed.

KL: Dick Gregory doesn't forget St. Louis [his childhood home], and he doesn't forget what he came from. He is a man who also has persisted in identifying himself with the people who are pretty far down on the ladder of trying to find their place as American citizens.

DG: Mississippi has laws on the book today, laws aimed at the Negro. White America has been sitting back and watching these laws be aimed at the Negro. One such law requires the name of anyone registering to vote must automatically appear in the local newspapers. Well, this is merely a method of intimidation. In other words, if I work for you on your plantation, and if I decide to slip into town to register to vote, within a matter of two to three days, you will find out about it and you can decide to fire me.

KL: To what extent is this followed up with violence?

DG: In one case, a Negro and his family of twelve is put off the plantation completely. In another instance, a Negro is shot at—they shoot at his home. There are instances where a Negro minister will try to organize voter registration, and people will go so far as to burn down his church.

Can you imagine what kind of protection a Negro has in a town where he is bucking the system and the Chief of Police is the President of the White Citizen Council? [Audience laughter] The worst, frightening feeling I have ever had in my life was when I was in Greenwood, Mississippi [to participate in a demonstration there]. It dawned on me one night, that if anybody tried to do me bodily harm, not even connected to racial desegregation demonstrations—just bodily harm; I couldn't even call the police [for help].

KL: Wouldn't you encourage the Negro in the South to stay down there, rather than go to the [inhospitable] North?

DG: In the South there is a much healthier situation for the Negro than in the North. Of course the Negro runs the risk of being lynched in the South. Up North they will give him a job for a dollar an hour and starve him to death, so it's really no difference. The White Southerner is honest with the Negro, the Barnetts [Gov. of Mississippi], the Wallaces, [Gov. of Alabama], the Faubuses [Gov. of Arkansas]—they all tell [us] what we can do and what we cannot do. Up North they tell you one thing and you find out later that it is something else. Truth is a heck of a force even if it is misused.

KL: Do you see an advantage though at least in this in the North? You implied previously I guess that you can call the police.

DG: If the Mississippi power structure would go to New York City or go to Chicago or to any northern city, it would study their system and carry it back to Mississippi; they could keep the Negro down for another two to three hundred years.

KL: You said that you aren't likely to find many bitter Negroes as you travel through the South. You wouldn't begin to imply by this that they are happy?

DG: All of your Negro leadership [today] are products of the South, so a Negro up North very, very seldom gets to see a Negro in authority. I am not advocating segregated schools, but in a segregated school in the South you have a Negro principal and the Negro in the South at a very early age gets to see a Negro in authority.

This scene does not exist up North. The Negro in the South has a purpose, has a meaning, and all he wants is freedom. He will eventually free himself and the South will eventually free the northern Negro and eventually the White man in America will become free.

KL: You stopped me for a minute when you said, "Free the White man," I think we Whites have pretty well gotten the idea that we are free right now, man.

DG: The only thing the southern White man has to identify with is a washroom. He has a separate toilet and he has fought so hard to keep a separate toilet, he has forgotten to ask for a clean one. Every time we integrate a library in the South, there are ten thousand Whites who did not know that library had [even] existed. Had they known this, the library would have been larger in the first place.

We Negroes up North have always been looking down on the Negroes in the South, particularly the Negro in Mississippi; and when someone up North would call us a nigger, we would make ourselves believe that it was this one in Mississippi responsible for the stereotypes ascribed to us – all the kinky hair, all the big lips, and splitting all the verbs. Then when you look around one day and your whipping boy is rising up, saying, "This is what I want you to give me!" This is what started from [demonstrations in] Greenwood, Mississippi, and Birmingham.

KL: Yeah, but don't you see this, that a good many White people are concerned about this, Dick?

DG: I would say 99.9% of White America up North wants to see the Negro with equal rights, but he is not too stuck on integration. [Audience laughter] On the plantation [down South], you see the big White house where the master lives and about two hundred yards behind this White house you would see a shack where the Negro sharecropper lives: Two hundred yards behind the White mansion.

We can't live this close to White people up North. With a Negro family living two hundred yards behind that White mansion, when this Negro's kid gets sick in the middle of the night and he cries, that Mississippi White man hears him. Up North, you don't know if our kid died in his sleep until we come to work [next morning] and tell you about it. Now with me living two hundred yards in the back of your home in Mississippi, and I have been there for twenty five years, we have talked about a lot of things. We have been honest about a lot of things.

KL: Don't you really think that the church still is a power that can begin to do something here?

DG: If it's not too late, I think for some strange reason or another the "Power Above" has waited for two hundred years for the church to pick up the ball; and it was wide open for two hundred years and then we had the Civil War and then a hundred more years [passed]. It would have been a great thing had the church, [somewhere in all these years], stepped forward with leadership; it would have been a feather in God's cap, because we would have said, "Thank God." But the church has failed in such a horrible way that now everyone seems to say, "Thank the Supreme Court."

KL: But what can we say to a group [of young people] like this waiting for marching orders from the Lord and willing to say, "I am ready to go, but what about in this [matter of race relations]? I really feel pretty helpless!"

DG: I don't know; it's almost too late to say anything now. Unless we are willing to learn and to understand (which is very hard to do in a few minutes), what parents before us couldn't understand and couldn't learn in a hundred years. When a man has truth and right on his side, one man can go up against an army and win.

KL: We hear you saying that the commodity that you possess and believe in is what you call and describe as truth—that this is the great big power that you have embraced. We think that the institutional church, the organization, has pushed truth aside often enough, but we still think that the people who are truly God's church have this commodity and this is what we want desperately to hang on to—the kind of commodity that says that God loves people and that God has made you [and all of us to be].

That God has had the same kind of love essentially for you, the same potential to be [a force] in His kingdom and in this world. But when people frustrate what God intends, they violate His truth. Now we would like to capture [and harness] this truth. This is what we feel we can throw our lot in with and this we must do.

DG: The right we are fighting for is this same Constitution that certain people are trying to use against us. If this Constitution is right and the beautiful document which peoples all over the world believe it is, we cannot lose by using it right. If the Cuban rebels defeated Castro tonight, they would cheer. We have never picked up one gun, one stick, no dynamite. We have never said, "Let's go downtown and take over city hall." We said, "We are going to take our body and lay it on the line for right; all at once." The Negro in America has decided that he would rather die trying to be free than to live as a slave, this is all – no more, no less. [And Whites will say] say, "But what about my neighborhoods?" What about them?

Two hundred years you have depreciated my soul and I don't give a damn about your grass. My soul is much more important than your dirt. We are going to come into these White schools and the most frightening thing in the world is to listen to people say, "Well what about the standards of my schools?" Good schools have always flunked out stupid people; stupid people have never busted out schools. So when that Negro moves into the neighborhood and moves into the school, if the neighborhood crumbles and the school crumbles: You have been living in a myth all along. And people sit by, they have a bi-racial committee. It's as if this room caught on fire right now and we decided to pick out a number of you to sit up here and decide what we're gonna do about it [Audience laughter]. Now you know the only thing to do is to open up these exits and clean this room out as peacefully and orderly as we can in good faith. This is what it amounts to today; the Negro wants his equal rights, every White man in America knows what the Negro wants and when he says, "Come into my office" actually what he is saying is, "Come into my office and let me find out at what point can I pacify you." Well, baby, this house is on fire and we're gonna get out!

(The following seven paragraphs were not included in the recorded version)

[To no one's surprise, someone rose first to ask "What about interracial marriage?"]

KL: The Christian's role is not to be judge, to determine the "rightness" or "wrongness" of transracial marriage. Such marriages already exist – their families begun. The reality confronting us as Christians: "Do we have loving concern for these young couples – and for the children in these families?"

All marriages sooner or later encounter some difficulties. The ultimate difficulty all couples will encounter is death: death in the family, death of the partner. It is the assignment of the Christian community to be supportive, affirming, understanding, helpful. It would be a decidedly unchristian thing to distance ourselves from any wedded pair—and/or their children.

We ought to take notice today how few of the three thousand people at this convention are Black.

In these past few years the Lutheran Church has experienced a spectacular growth in membership, due largely to a spirit of outreach and welcome. The increase in numbers, however, has been, for the most part, among White people.

An estimated 19,000 Blacks hold membership in our church. Had we similarly been welcoming Blacks to our roster of members at that same rate, we would now on this day have 229,000 Negro members in our church.

We have learned that some of our Lutheran congregations have publicly announced "We will accept into membership any Negro who would like to join us, but we are not going to go out and recruit Negroes for membership."

Person One from audience (female): If the educational opportunities for both the Negro and the White race were the same and if the White schools were integrated, do you feel that after a certain period of time both races would separate and attend their own schools?

DG: Well, this is a law of nature. The Baptists will go to the Baptist convention, the Methodists will go to the Methodist convention, and the Lutherans will go to the Lutherans' convention until someone says in the Baptist convention, "We don't want no Methodists and no Lutherans."

Person Two (black, female): You talked about the bitterness before, don't you think that that could be the Negro's fault too? Coming up into the North they can't expect us to move right in and be a part of all of this?

DG: This is almost like saying if a man cuts me and I bleed, isn't this my fault that I am bleeding? Well if you have a tea kettle or a coffee pot sitting on a stove and you build this pressure up in this coffee pot. That pot is going to blow one day and you can blame the tea kettle if you want, but you better get out of the way. [Audience laughter]

Person Three (male, white): Talking about the riots again, I am worried about that. When the riots start, the Negro might not care what that White person feels because he is White; and if he is going to stand in the way, whether that White person loves the Negro or not, he is going to get it.

DG: You are not in half the amount of danger as that light complexioned Negro that looks White; this is the guy that I feel sorry for. This is the one that will be killed by his own. When we go to war against enemy troops, they have certain uniforms and when you see it you shoot. A race riot is such a brutal thing, because the only uniform you see is a color. It's White against Black and if this thing blows, the White cop on the beat and the Negro cop on the beat, if it breaks big enough both of these individuals will go home and protect their family.

Bring in the soldiers; there will be no soldiers, because this will be the first time in the history [of] race riots in this country that we have had an integrated army. They will be fighting back at the barracks, now what will happen? You would not participate in a race riot; I would not participate in a race riot. So while the riot is going on you will stay in your home and I will stay in my home. But if this riot lasts longer than two weeks, now the two of us have to come out of our house to get some food. The riot is still going on; you that had no intentions of participating must go out and get food for the family. You are going to take your gun and I am going to take mine; this is why a riot in 1963 would be so dangerous.

KL: I'm concerned about whether or not we can still get the kind of message across that Roy Wilkens of the NAACP gave down in Charleston, South Carolina, last week. Wilkens said, "Please don't forget we are going to have to live with these people after it's over."

DG: This is very beautiful—if you had someone on your side saying the same thing. We haven't blown up one White church. We haven't shot into one White home. And in three hundred years in this country we have never lynched a White man.

KL: We know that people have now been released on bail to the tune of one and four tenths million dollars, which is an awful lot of money, especially when taken from people with meager financial resources.

DG: I've been asked many times whether my involvement with the civil rights struggle hurt me financially. My true honest answer is, I don't know. I would rather starve to death helping anyone who is fighting for decent, common rights with truth on their side than to live a rich man, a wealthy man without it. It is just that simple.

Abraham Lincoln summed it up when he said, real simple and real sweet: "I would never be a slave; therefore I could never be a master." I don't want you to think for one minute I am here as a Negro telling you what you better do. I am here as an individualist first, an American second, and a Negro third. And I am just trying to give you free what I have bought and paid for. I am not forcing it on you, because there is one great force in truth. You do not have to believe it, but history will write the final chapter. Thank you so much.

KL: I think you know a little bit about what I said before, that this guy, Mr. Dick Gregory, is one of the most religious men I have ever met. In that sense I express gratitude not only to him but to God for the chance to have him as part of our convention.

Person Four (female): I think that we were discussing amongst our group what Reverend Witt meant when he said that he thought that Dick Gregory was an extremely religious person.

KL: He was right; Pastor Witt did not say that he was a very Lutheran man; he did not say he was a very Christian man. This man has deep convictions about a concern for his fellow man and he pursues his conviction with commitment and passion religiously and this is what Pastor Witt meant.

Person Five (male): I would like to know what you people think about interracial marriages.

Person Six (male): Unless we as the Christian Church can accept in love one of the offspring of an integrated marriage, it's going to be hard for this marriage to succeed.

Person seven (male): In the scripture off hand I think of two cases of marriages that we might call interracial and you cannot prove or I cannot prove from the scripture that interracial marriages are wrong.

KL: I am not so sure that this is a normal process that we are being asked: whether a certain marriage is right or wrong or if it makes any difference. In America, we are finding that the situation does occur. Now when we say this isn't a good thing, this is bad, be careful. I think we ought to do everything we possibly can when we find a marriage that looks difficult, to help these people stay together.

I found it kind of strange that we were able to accept what a fellow panelist said just a few minutes ago, that if the church isn't ready to accept the children of a mixed marriage, it might be very hard. I think we better ask ourselves some serious questions. What is wrong with the Christian who doesn't want to accept certain children? It may be true that the children of an interracial marriage aren't going to be accepted in certain pockets in the Negro community or in certain pockets in the White community or in the vast majority of cases. But in the Christian church we have the opportunity to bid ALL people welcome in the name of our Lord Christ.

Person eight (female White): Why is it even here at this convention there are so few Negroes as Walther Leaguers?

Person nine (male White): How can we praise God in everything and still almost ignore this question?

Person ten (male White): You might just think–well– that this is something that just people in the South have to worry about because there are no Negroes that live by me so why should I care? But it should be the interest of everyone, but what to do about it?

Person eleven (female Black): You said a few minutes ago that you don't want these demonstrations, but we would like to wait just as much as anybody else would and we have prayed, but we have waited a long time. It's all right what we are doing, we don't go out for violence but we have waited so long, we try to do things peacefully and we always get these beautiful speeches about what's going to happen.

We wait and they say to stop demonstrating and when we stop demonstrating nothing happens. What we need is for as many White people to come out as possible to the demonstrations. You who live in the South can really help us, because if a few of you come and it would give others the courage to come out.

Person twelve (female Black): I always wondered now if I go here will they just look at me and force a smile, try be nice or something like that or would they accept me just as a Walther Leaguer or something without wondering whether I am a Negro or White. Well today I am convinced it is good to be here and I just wanted to say that everyone here has just been wonderful and I want to thank everyone here.

KL: One reason that there aren't more Negro Lutherans present at this meeting is because, if we had the outreach in the Negro communities that was at a par with the outreach in the White communities, we would now instead of having sixteen thousand Negro Lutheran communicants in our church, we would have two hundred twenty nine thousand. And still we hear some churches bravely saying, "We have opened our doors so that now if a Negro wants to come, he can come in naturally, but we won't go out of our way to get someone in." This doesn't sound too much like the spirit of our Lord, Christ, who said, "Go out into the highway and byway; be what God has made you to be, his alive child who has received the love of God and who is now to pass that love on."

The only thing that keeps us from enjoying God's full love to give unto others is fear. Some people don't want to invite Negroes to church because they are afraid of interracial marriage; afraid they might become too good friends, they are afraid their real estate values would go down. I think it is about time we understand our Lord has called us not to fear, we have been freed to love fully.

[End of transcript]

The 3,500 Walther Leaguers who, gathered in convention in 1963, in the ballroom of the Sheraton Park Hotel in Washington D.C., had the unforgettable experience of hearing one of the most unusual voices of the day share his personal perspectives on one of our country's most vital issues in its history.

And one week after this event with Dick Gregory, in this same city, the March on Washington was held.

Under Elmer Witt's leadership, the Walther League was winning the appreciation and respect of the church for the role the League was filling in reaching out in its concern for the very young Lutherans of the country.

Concordia Seminary in St. Louis, recognizing the significant contribution Elmer Witt had been making during his tenure, designated him as recipient of an honorary doctorate.

Dr. Oliver Harms, who was President of the LCMS at the time, wrote him a congratulatory letter, commenting that such degrees more often than not simply attest to the recipient's worthiness of recognition, a bestowal of respect and honor. "In your case, this is no mere 'honorary' degree—this is an earned, much deserved degree, recognizing your wise and faithful service to the church and our Lord."

In that favorable atmosphere, the Synod also asked Elmer to head up its Board for Young People's Work. While that decision provided financial relief for the League, the arrangement also put his work in a vulnerable position. He was now accountable to the Synod.

That meant that though he was still executive officer of the Walther League, a portion of his salary would now be borne by the LCMS. He became officially attached to the structured church and no longer merely head of a "voluntary organization." So, instead of functioning somewhat independently in a setting conducive to free, constructive, and creative development of programs, he found himself in an increasingly confining position and subject to sharply criticizing voices censuring his leadership.

There were detractors of the League's endeavors to help youth understand the role of Christians in a world torn by an increasingly unpopular Viet Nam War, explosive rioting in the inner cities, fear of communist invasion, the assassination of our president, disruption on University campuses.

A significantly loud chorus of churchly voices–pastors especially, but laity, too–sharply attacked the League's program, threatening to withdraw congregational support for the Synod's overall budget. Though a minority of congregations participated in this bitter stand, this organized opposition effectively caused eventual withdrawal of Synodical financial support and ultimately resulted in the wilting and fading of the League and its vigorous, venturous, and faithful ministry.

For a later convention, Elmer and his staff invited folk singer Pete Seeger. Although Seeger's appearance was well-received by those who attended the convention, protests from assailants proved effective and played a lead role in characterizing Seeger as left wing, unpatriotic, un-Lutheran, and ultimately an inappropriate invitee to a meeting of Lutheran youth.

This proved to be one of the key issues that undermined Elmer's ministry with the Walther League and ultimately caused the League to crumble.

Subsequently, Elmer accepted a post with a Lutheran Youth Research program in Minneapolis while maintaining a family home in Matteson, Illinois, some fifty miles to the west of the our home in Valparaiso. This proved a bridge for his moving into two other phases of his career —the first of these as campus pastor at Governor's State University, a community college not far from the Witts' Matteson home. He later served as director of Holden Village, a retreat center, once a mining community in the Cascade Mountains of Washington state.

A Tribute to Ginny Witt

I remember a house full of kids doubling up on sleeping space and lots of running up and down to the basement, which often seemed the arena in which a full schedule of play happened. With Elmer frequently absent, Ginny became the orchestrator of a long list of games and projects to busy the five vibrantly bright and imaginative young minds of the Witt kids who filled her life day after day and all the evenings between.

Particularly vivid to me are my rememberings of our visits to her in her last days. I remember her telling of her engaging clergy—type folk—two among these: Dr. Joseph Sitler and Dr. Martin Marty—in conversations about "after death," and she would sort of chuckle at the inadequacy of people to envision what such an important climax of the Christian journey would be. And she would, with a broad smile, comment that she would be learning all about these matters long before these theologian friends of hers.

Ginny's condition had come to the point where she was unable to eat any food—her diet was reduced to the point that she was limited to lemon popsicles.

As her hours among us became shorter and fewer, Elmer and their young ones were gathered around her bed, when one of them asked, "Mom, is there anything we can do, anything you'd like?"

Her surprising response: "I'd like some pizza and beer!" They were astonished and amused. Knowing her and her sharp wit, they might have expected that kind of comment. She said, "I'm serious —I suppose you think it wouldn't be good for my health?"

They complied with her wish and served her. She ate with gusto—and of course, the fare didn't stay with her. She insisted, however, that it had been wonderful.

We drove over to the Witt home in Matteson to see her again—it was our last visit with her. She was alone in the house, but the rear door of the house was open, so we entered. And there she was, sitting up at her little desk, pen in hand. She had been attending to some of the medical bills that had arrived. Now she was addressing envelopes so that notes to friends might be ready for the family to send out when she would reach life's end.

She said simply, "Life goes on, you know." Trite saying—but profound words in this setting—and especially when spoken by Ginny.

Elmer's Retirement

Late one night—years before Elmer began his work in youth ministry—he called me. His voice was excited as he spoke, asking me to perform his marriage to Ginny. And that I did, only a few weeks later. Not many months after they had wed, and after he had begun directing the program of the International Walther League, Elmer began to realize the many miles of travel that were being required of him. Among the first of the many trips he'd be making was to a meeting to be held in Denmark. Ginny was to go with him, so they were now facing the responsibility of providing care for their four young ones, especially during their overseas travels.

Ginny's sister had agreed to keep Tom (the youngest) and Barb during the parents' absence, and the parents were now asking Esther and me whether Anne (the eldest of the four) and Paul (the liveliest) might stay with us. Because the Lutze and the Witt kids got along so very well with one another, we readily agreed to help out. As details for carrying out the arrangement and plans were crystallizing, it occurred to Ginny and Elmer that they had made no provisions for care of their children, should any accident occur that would leave the children parentless.

They made a personal call to us and asked whether we would be willing to accept the guardianship of their four should any tragic accident deprive their children of their parents. This was not a situation to be taken on lightly. Aside from all other considerations, the thought of voluntarily taking on full accountability for the safety, the care, and well-being of four children—in addition to our own—was altogether sobering.

There really was, of course, no other choice, and with prayer, we agreed to say, "Yes." Esther and I often reflected on that decision, and always with gratitude that such dire circumstances never occurred.

When Elmer retired from his role at Holden, he moved to a small home in Tacoma. After Ginny's death, his children had scattered and were pursuing their own careers. To offset his loneliness, Elmer traveled much, visiting country-wide among the many friends he had accumulated through the years. One he discovered, however, lived in a community close by his Tacoma home.

Friendship with Phyllis Brandt had found its roots in earlier days. She was now a teacher, but when younger, had been one of the talented youth who served as Walther League Caravaners. Again I was asked to perform a wedding—that of Elmer Witt to Phyllis Brandt.

Shortly before Christmas, years later, I received a call from Paul. Elmer was on a respirator and it was soon to be removed. Paul handed the phone to his father. I spoke a few words to Elmer, and said goodbye to my longtime friend.

Elmer Witt and Karl Lutze, lifelong friends.

CHAPTER 3

WALT REINER

E arlier I promised to tell a bit more about my friend Walt Reiner. Let me keep my promise here. I first met him at one of the Walther League's national conventions—this one on campus in Oxford, Ohio. I had not yet moved to Valparaiso, and although I had an increased amount of responsibilities back in Oklahoma at our rapidly growing church in Tulsa, I agreed to take on what amounted to "dean of students" role at that meeting, supervising a group of adults whose chief concern would be the direct care of the more than 2,000 youth who would be attending the convention, housed in the University's residence halls, as well as supervising and coordinating the smaller group study sessions.

Elmer Witt recognized the dimensions of this assignment and therefore had already engaged Professor Walt Reiner of Valparaiso University's faculty to assist me. Walt was in Valpo's Athletic Department. In addition to classroom responsibilities, he was also football and track coach. Although we had never met before, I had already found favor with him a few years earlier.

Floyd Henderson, an exceptionally fine athlete, attended the church I served in Oklahoma. He was a star on the local high school's football team. I recommended his contacting Valpo U. whose staff not only awarded him an athletic scholarship, but in his very first game, saw him return a kickoff for a touchdown.

Walt, I found, was chosen to work with me because he had recently been named by Valpo President Kretzmann to design and administer a new program at the school to be called the Youth Leadership Training Program (YLTP). Students who enrolled in the new program themselves found the title a bit cumbersome and early on chose to shorten the title of the new academic offering, naming it " YLTP," or if you spoke the letters fast enough, reduced them to sound like "Wild Teepee."

The entire concept demonstrated the—here I grope for the right word—skills? genius? vision? brilliance? wisdom? of O.P. Kretzman.

This was a time when "Mother Church" (the LCMS) had little time—or money!—for a school that was not producing "workers for the kingdom." Lutheran congregations that had participated in the original purchase of the University were expecting a return on their investment and shouldn't be "over-solicited." In their minds, its purpose was to cope with and, indeed, use to advantage the culture of energy and young people in an area in which most pastors could use help.

What a moment for Valparaiso to be identifying some of the church's brightest and best young people for roles of leadership and service. And, though the program would be administered under the Theology Department, O.P. selected as Director a refreshing person whom everyone on campus called, "Coach," a winsome, hard-working, and creative, practical guy.

When he had come to Valpo as track coach and found the school had no track, he'd go right from classroom each day to the maintenance department to borrow the University's truck and a shovel. He'd arranged for removing cinders piled near the Pennsy Railroad tracks a half mile away and laid a regulation-size track for his runners. This "can-do" spirit marked Walt's career at Valparaiso.

Long after the success of the Ohio Walther League convention and as the YLTP program was performing beyond expectations, Walt was noting how the government chose to engage youth of the day in its Peace Corps program. He was ready for a new venture. Both the VU administration and the Walther League supported him in launching "Prince of Peace Volunteers," a program which assigned students to year-long internships in Lutheran parishes located in troubled metropolitan centers of the country. Walt and family moved to Chicago for three years. The program expanded to be named the "Prince of Peace Corps," tying students with overseas community service programs, primarily in Japan.

During those days, Walt would spend days with students in Chicago and also tend to administration of his programs from offices in the downtown quarters of the Walther League. As I remember, it was a Friday evening and the staff was in good spirits, closing shop. The Reiner family was preparing to move back to Valparaiso.

Before leaving, Barbara Cotton, an African-American employed by the League, had an unusual response to Walt's congenial, "Have a good weekend, Barbara!"

"Thanks, and you have a nice weekend in your lovely suburban Valparaiso while I go back to our home near Cabrini Green."

Cabrini Green was a public housing community of multi-storied buildings on Chicago's near-North Side, over-crowded and under-serviced with a reputation as undesirable, repulsive, and dangerous.

Conceding that there were many advantages to living in Valparaiso, Walt started to list instances of resistance to Blacks coming there for employment—and far more as residents. She certainly wouldn't want to expose herself or her family to that kind of confrontation and the accompanying pains that attend such blatant rejection.

To this, Mrs. Cotton answered that Blacks are used to being told that by White people, as if Whites always think they know what the Negro's preferences might be. She challenged him further: how could he know how a single mother with a family of six felt when she had to return at night to an area where there's shooting, drinking, and drugs all around?

Promising to explore the matter with her the following week, Walt's mind was spinning—and troubled.

Next day already, back at Valparaiso, he'd gathered a handful of neighbors—university people and church folk—for coffee and conversation. Walt wasn't about to turn his back on Mrs. Cotton and after hearing him out, it was clear that we weren't about to do so either. There were some bright and creative minds around the room. They came up with ideas of her moving to Valparaiso balanced by a realistic listing of obstacles such a move would encounter.

We parted our ways, agreeing to host Barbara in a visit to Valpo so she could make a judgment to determine for herself if she would like to move to this very, very White community.

Walt's wife, Loie, his ever warm and spirited "welcome personified" partner (even on the icy bleachers on frigid Saturdays when Walt's team was on the football field!) agreed to bring Barbara to Valparaiso for a brief visit. They introduced her to some of the very few African-American students enrolled at the University, who readily reported on negative experiences they'd had while on campus.

At the city's new and well-equipped Lutheran elementary school, she had an opportunity to converse with its principal and a few teachers. They offered the Cotton children a tuition-free scholarship and cheery welcome, were they to enroll. No need to say more or look farther. She loved it. No way could we walk away now.

Then the problems began. She was in no position to go out house-shopping. Walt reconvened all of us who had been at the earlier meeting. With only the experience we'd each had in buying houses for ourselves when we had first come to Valparaiso, we pooled our limited perspectives and tried to find a house for Barbara and her family in Valparaiso.

Phone calls and face-to-face visits with local real estate agents proved unproductive. Invariably we found them polite and receptive until they learned that the house we were looking for was intended for Black occupants. Most saw us as extremely naïve. A few even commended us as noble or idealist, but confessed their fear that if they were to be the first "to bring colored folk to our community [which has been so successful in keeping them out!]," it could ruin their trade. A few even assured us that if some other real estate firm would work with us and be the first to complete such a transaction, they'd be glad–and quick–to be second! As a matter of fact, even after Barbara had been the first, we still found it impossible to find any real estate agency willing to find a home for the second new arrivals.

Everyone in our little group had endorsed the failed effort. The next step seemed to call for our reporting to Mrs. Cotton, "See, Barbara, as Walt told you earlier, you wouldn't want to live in a place that so flagrantly has made its position clear, 'We don't want people of color here."

Indefatigable Walt wouldn't settle for that.

The coach went into a huddle with Loie, his loyal, wonderfully gutsy wife and partner and emerged to share with the team his end-around play to circumvent the obstacles confronting them. The Reiner's home at the bottom of the hill on Cedar Lane had been built on an oversized lot. Walt told the group that he and Loie had thought through the entire matter and decided to donate a significantly large slice of the property for the purpose of building a house there for the Cotton family,

The group was slightly overwhelmed by the generous offer. Salaries at the University were hardly impressively high, but the discussions finally began to crystallize. A few of the participants offered to mortgage their homes to meet necessary costs as the project would be launched. It took several more meetings to carve out a plan that would finally blossom into a house for Barbara.

To begin, we found Peter Knobel in one of Chicago's western suburbs, a contractor and a thoughtful, generous, young man who volunteered to coordinate the various steps encountered on the way to completing the project.

However, we had not really anticipated the systemic way the power people of the city would attempt to obstruct us as we proceeded.

Of course, we had to apprise the city officials, applying first for a building permit. Other obstacles materialized. We would have to tap onto the main water line approximately the length of a football field away from our site. That was not a surprise. When building our own homes a few years earlier, two of us had also been required to get water to our residences from the same line, about the same distance away, as had the Reiners. The pipe required was iron, one inch in diameter. However, for the home of this new Black resident, the pipe was to be three inch copper, putting the price tag prohibitively high. Solution: we were forced to install a well for the new house. And although the three aforementioned houses were located on an unpaved, single-lane road, the city required that the stretch immediately in front of the property provided by the Reiners be paved as a two-lane street, replete with cement curbing—even though the road ended at that point without exit to any other road or access to any highway or thoroughfare.

For design, we settled for a pre-cut attractive little cottage, the tentative owners named on official documents as Lutheran Builders. The home was erected by volunteers who gave long hours to the project—many of them members of Immanuel Lutheran Church or students and employees of the Lutheran University. Then, in order to welcome recruits from other groups, the name of the venturesome group of volunteers was changed to Valparaiso Builders.

The scene was exciting. A biology prof wielding a hammer, a theologian wrapping his wrench around a plumbing joint, faculty wives rolling paint on bedroom walls, neighborhood teenagers pitching in by lugging sheet rock panels through the open door ways, the University's business manager half way up a ladder lugging a bundle of shingles. Calloused hands and Band-Aids, grunting, and great satisfaction were the rewards of being involved.

When the building had become livable, the Cottons moved in. Some of the local citizenry were not opposed to African-Americans moving in and, in fact, were really appreciative that at long last the ice of frigid inhospitality had been broken, but they themselves were a bit wary and fearful of being personally involved.

There were threatening phone calls. One of the many rumors afloat accused "that guy Reiner" of planning a move of 400 Black families into Valparaiso. To assure the new residents safety and quiet for sleeping, each night people took turns staying in the little, temporary work cabin—sort of headquarters for the operation. All night long someone would be there with lamp, telephone, and coffee while they kept watch.

Living near Walt and Loie was always very special. Our children grew up together and our friendship grew stronger each year.

In about 1993 when I was home alone, I received a surprising phone call from Walt. I had been with him only a short time before, giving him a hand in moving an excessively heavy, oversized sliding door someone had bestowed on him for use in some remodeling project. He sounded almost panicky as he described his pain. I ran down the hill to be with him. Medical help and ambulance service arrived and as swiftly as possible, he was in the care of a heart surgeon.

After his recovery from surgery, he was ordered to walk for exercise. Walt and I would often go off together. We would usually drive to different more remote parts of the city, park the car, and explore neighborhoods we'd never known before. These gave occasion for conversation and discussion of topics ranging from prospects for the next football season to the writings of philosopher Jacque Elul. I looked forward to these sessions together.

Walt and Loie were there for Esther and me when Esther was diagnosed with cancer and her subsequent illness. The support of their visits gave Esther and me strength and comfort. When Esther was no longer with me, I met Gail and when we married in 1996, it was the Reiners who welcomed Gail into the circle of our friendship.

In September of 2002, while a cardiologist was administering a stress test on me, the screen attached to the instrument went wild and he stopped the procedure. He explained that I needed an angiogram. After this procedure, he scheduled me for open heart surgery.

I went home to wait, with instructions to do nothing. I was all for that. As I sat helplessly in my recliner, the family gathered around. And I knew that in the wings were our good friends, Loie and Walt. The wait was about four days. One afternoon Walt came in, bearing a branch about 10 inches long. "This is from the apple tree that is between our homes. That tree fell down last winter, as I was walking over here, I saw it was still living. It's a survivor. Just like you and me. You're going to make it."

Gail put that little branch in water and kept it for months. And when the surgery was taking place, good friend Loie showed up with muffins and fruits and lots of love to share with the gathered family. As I said, "They're family."

The surgery went well. I was still unsteady on my feet when my prescribed regimen called for short walks. My six-year-old grandson, Matthew, would take my hand and walk me down the road a few steps. And we both got to know each other and talked about what was happening in our lives.

When I was a bit more mobile and could walk greater distances, Walt would sometimes join me on my walks. And now, as I need a cane to walk, I have the one he left behind.

If you were to drop in at our house on Old Orchard Lane and wander down the steps to our grandkids' play area, you'd see mounted on the paneled stair wall an enlarged photo of all six of the Reiners: Mark, Becky, Pat, Beth, and Walt and Loie.

From time to time people have asked about replacing the photo featuring another theme, other than the Reiners.

Response: "They're neighbors—family; they stay!"

* * * * *

In 1996, Walt and I were both honored by Valparaiso University in receiving the Dr. Martin Luther King Award at the MLK Day celebration. Receiving the

Karl Lutze and Walt Reiner

award was very special; receiving it with Walt was even more so.

Walt was the voice of justice for the neighborhood. He continued to help us all see and help those in need. The Valparaiso Builders projects helped eight mothers and their children from inner city Chicago have homes in Valparaiso and helped the citizens of Valparaiso learn to live with folks they had known little about. Valparaiso Builders took a few years break and then was regrouped as Project Neighbors which continues to work to provide affordable housing for all people.

Walt had a number of "brushes with death". He had told us a little about his World War II experiences and landing on Normandy Beach. And he had fallen from a few rooftops doing work with Project Neighbors.

His call to me in 1993 had been due to a heart failure and there were subsequent heart events. There was one time—December of 2001 that we visited him at Rush Hospital in Chicago on Christmas Day. He looked so frail that as we left, Gail and I both felt we had said a final goodbye to our good friend. But a few months later, he was back at the Project Neighbors meetings—a bit weaker in body but as strong in spirit as ever.

When finally, on Dec 5, 2006, he said goodbye to all of us, a void was left in Valparaiso that none of us expect to be filled. On December 29, 2006, Walt's 83rd birthday, we all gathered to celebrate the gift of his life to us.

Walt and Karl at Karl's 85th.

CHAPTER 4
ESTHER

I n an attempt to complete a gathering of names, people, events, places, situations, and experiences that shaped my days and years of ministry, I will of course have omitted some that would have prompted my adding more pages to what resembles my autobiography. And that makes me uncomfortable, because readers may miss seeing names cited who themselves have helped shape my life and work.

So now it is time to remember and talk about Esther Marjory Lutze.

Esther Marjory Lutze

When we came to Valparaiso with the four boys in 1959, Mark was four years old, Tom was eight, Steve was 10, and Peter was 13. Obviously Esther was very busy with raising four boys, while I was extremely busy as a beginning professor and the new Field Secretary for LHRAA. As the boys grew, the family became involved in campus and town life.

Esther assisted in the LHRAA office part-time for many years, and also became the beloved mentor for many of the university women—students as well as staff.

Her earlier years had been preparing her for her "life-work." In our four years of courtship, it became clearer and clearer that her career might well unfold as being a clergy-wife—a multifaceted role of secretary, receptionist, administrative assistant, office manager, critic, wife, mother, orchestrator, and chief officer of domestic affairs. (Or, as Professor Fred Niedner put it, "Mother Teresa!")

There were so many more assignments and responsibilities. These became altered and expanded and in some instances narrowed and intensified as my own career roles developed. She adapted to these challenges exceptionally well.

Well known to the chapel staff by then, Esther was called upon to be a counselor and to assist with the chapel's residential ministry.

This was a perfect fit for a woman who had a great love of students. One example of this was her annual banana split. Clean rain gutters were stretched across the beautiful courtyard that joined Guild and Memorial residences for women. Bananas and gallons upon gallons of ice cream filled the gutters and at a signal, the women would rush from the dorms to add their chosen toppings to the waiting banana splits. This was a final exam treat that is a fond memory for hundreds of students. Creative, yes, but also a natural for the woman who would bake brownies and send them with her husband for his students to nibble on as they wrote their final exams.

Some 48 years after our marrying, she was smitten by a rare type of cancer that in the months that followed, enveloped the nerve cells near the brain. We had had the very best of surgeons and their medical teams who could be found in the Midwest. In spite of their efforts, the malady ruthlessly reduced her well-being and ultimately robbed her of her mobility and capacity to perform even some of the simplest self-care tasks.

Esther wrestled with the frustrations that attended her awareness that her performance in almost every aspect of her life had so significantly diminished. While Esther was still at home, we would welcome days and nights when our lives centered in living room space, where the large reclining chair like a magnet drew all of us around that chair's occupant, Esther.

Her primary change of position was provided by her wheelchair and, at night, her bed down the hall proved a refuge from sameness.

A welcome variety in scenery was the parade of caring folks who found their way to our door to show their love and, often to rue their helplessness in not being able to do more for Esther. More often than not, people would walk right in. But not wanting to be disruptive of any care the patient might be receiving at the moment, sometimes they'd ring the doorbell.

One day, as I was attending to some of her needs, I responded to the doorbell to find there a woman who introduced herself as Director of the Visiting Nurses Association.

She said simply, "I've come to meet this Mrs. Lutze myself. All of our staff people who have been coming to your home are always so eager to be assigned to care for her. You see," she explained, "our workers who go to private homes to attend to these physically limited patients are often rebuffed by the people they are there to care for and their families—people who are themselves experiencing difficult days—but Mrs. Lutze makes our staff feel so good and appreciated for the services they provide. She's a real morale booster and our staff members love to serve her. I just want to meet her and thank her personally. She is very important to us."

In Esther's waning days and hours, her caring for and encouraging those serving her became her "life-work" and she performed well.

I was home a lot those days and found it a bit embarrassing to be pitied or pampered by visitors who didn't grasp the gratification that was mine in caring for this life mate who through the years—and even now in her time of extreme physical limitation—still showered me with love and care.

One more word about visitors during those days. Esther was always genuinely and deeply appreciative that in her house-boundness, friends would come by to show their care and, time after time, would comment about their frustration at not being able to do more for Esther. In fact they themselves derived so much from being with her—invigorated, refreshed, and enriched.

It's true, however that after the procession of caring friends tapered, she would often be fatigued—grateful, but exhausted. On one such night, Esther sighed and said, "That was nice, but that was enough."

After a few moments passed, she said, "You know, the Reiners weren't here today." Not five minutes later, the door opened and Walt's familiar football-field voice echoed through the house, "Anybody home? We're here!" You see, they're family. Longtime.

It was May of 1994. Esther was now in the hospital. For years she had been active in supporting the Lutheran Deaconess Association and was well loved by all the women. One afternoon Louise Williams, the director of the LDA, arrived with four other women. She told Esther how much they all loved her and how much they felt she was a part of the Deaconess program. Then she told her that the board had decided that Esther Lutze was a Deaconess and should be awarded the Deaconess pin.

Esther, who had not been speaking much, uttered a few words indicating her excitement. The women sang, said a prayer, and then began to say goodbye. Esther was obviously reluctant to let them go, but finally Louise said, "We have to leave; you need your rest."

For days, though conscious, Esther did not speak much. Her illness had well sapped her strength. Peter had spent the night alone at her side at the hospital, as had his brothers on the preceding nights. It was my turn now to take his place. As her eyes opened and her lips formed a warm smile, I held her hand. "Good morning, darling! Happy 49th Anniversary–and blessed Ascension Day (It was the 40th day after Easter)!"

For her to say even a word called for more strength and effort than she was able to muster, but her eyes sparkled.

I filled the silence of the moment with stories–about the time we met; about our long walks; about the chicks we raised in our kitchen. I reminded her of the birth of each of the four boys and our deciding what their names would be, and of our trips to Wisconsin to show them off to our folks. And our singing together in the St. Louis Bach Festivals while I was still a seminary student; the wonderful people in Oklahoma and colleagues and neighbors in Valparaiso, and the students dropping by our house. It had been a happy hour of remembering.

And I hushed. And she needed her sleep.

CHAPTER 5

WHAT'S AGING?

B efore people reach 50, they want to talk about challenges they are facing; after 50, they start comparing lists of medications they are taking for a variety of ailments. Along about my age—94—the best comments for launching a conversation prove to be our tales of surviving.

So let me tell you about this conversation with my dentist, who for well over 30 years, had been taking good care of me, but I halfway believe that whenever through the years I would come to his office, they turned on music softly, so I wouldn't hear it. The music I'm sure was the hymn tune *Crown Him With Many Crowns*. So indeed I have a royal mouthful.

My dentist's successor has told me that the crowns were good ones, but he sees the situation resembling a condition of asphalt poured into a pothole in a concrete highway. A crumbling occurs. So he persuaded me to replace the weakening residents in my oral cavity with implants. This was taking a long while and I'd had enough soup, yogurt, oatmeal, and other such soft goodies to last me the rest of my days. The whole process called for a lot of precise measuring and molding, construction, and laboratory work and I was almost finished with the process.

I was almost at the end of my multi-sessioned treatment and in one session, my dentist and his assistant were leaning over me. I was being a perfect patient. It's almost impossible to grumble anyway with fifteen or twenty fingers in my mouth, plus a tray on the side holding a variety of instruments to be used in the process, the automatic rinser, and who knows what else.

Things were going well when there was a sudden disruption. I sat up, coughed a bit and then both my professionals were obviously aghast. The tiny screwdriver, about 3/4 inch long and 1/8 inch in diameter was missing. It obviously had not fallen to the floor; it must have slipped down my throat.

Near panic prevailed. Meanwhile, I felt no discomfort, let alone pain. Gail whisked me off to the local hospital's emergency room, where the X-ray revealed that the metallic piece had not slipped down the digestive tract, but was lodged in a bronchial tube slightly above the lung. The emergency room doctor backed off from taking on my case and after inquiring of local surgeons whom to call on, we were told that our hospital had called Chicago University Hospital. Pulmonary specialists there had agreed to accept my case.

I was hustled off by ambulance to Chicago, Gail in the front seat with the driver. When we arrived in Chicago, more X-rays. The tool had not gone down pointed side first, so apparently no damage had been done to either pierce or scratch the bronchial tube.

The next day at 10 AM, the specialists and two staff members supervised the anesthesia process and were successful in removing the foreign object. They used state of the art exploration equipment and I could hear their elated comments as in triumph, they retrieved the invader.

A few hours later, Gail and I were on our way home, thanks to our good friends, the Balkos, coming to get us. The hospital asked for permission to keep the screwdriver for exhibit in medical classroom studies. (And perhaps, methinks, as a trophy as well.) We got a colored photo of the surgical process of inserting a tube that made the removal possible. Not having eaten for the previous two days, we were ready for and thoroughly enjoyed a big dinner with the musical Balkos.

Of course, we are grateful but there were no heroics involved on my part. No pain, no aftereffects whatsoever. Surely, reason for thanksgiving.

Maybe what I have written could be a bestseller if it were longer. Possible names: *Adventure with My Denture* or *I Swallowed a Screwdriver.*

PS—One of our friends who does carpentry repair work for us from time to time has warned us that he is keeping his lid on the tool box if I happen to be around where he is working.

CHAPTER 6
BEEN THERE, DONE THAT, NOT YET FINISHED

W hat I have recorded constitutes a sort of inventory of situations, events, and people. They help me look back in order that I might look ahead.

My credentials that might justify my discussing aging?

Well, first of all, I've had some personal exposure to the phenomenon of aging (you might categorize them as "case studies"):

- my father died in his 89th year;
- his sister Sophia at 94.
- my mother died at 93;
- her brother George at 95;
- each of my three sisters died shortly before reaching 92.

And, by the way, in case you haven't noticed, I'm not a young man—matter of fact, a short time from another birthday in the 90s. So, I've had opportunities for a bit of self-scrutiny.

The congregation to which I belong sponsors a monthly meeting for folks over 65. The program is called Elderjoy. They gather for a meal at a local restaurant, usually listen to someone invited to talk on a variety of subjects, they visit. They compete in a paper and pencil puzzle prepared for each session, and after singing "Happy Birthday" to all those whose birthdays fall in that month, they leave.

The people who attend are good folk. I do join them occasionally, but not frequently. It's not that I don't like these people. I do. I think I harbor resentment against the very idea of being regimented together with people on the basis of our "oldness."

Let me tell you, please, of another part of my past that I regard as vital in developing my understanding in the area of human longevity.

During my seminary classroom days, in anticipation of my future ministry, I had often envisioned myself devoting much time, energy—wherever I might eventually be stationed—to develop a strong program for involving youth in the life of the church.

So, after receiving my diploma and arriving on the scene of my first pastorate in Oklahoma, you can imagine my surprise when I discovered this congregation's short roster of members numbered only sixteen, eleven of whom were over 65. Seven of these were 75 or older. All of them were African-American. All of them had been living in poverty all their days. Five of them could neither read nor write. Some of them were grandchildren of former slaves. They were, in the truest sense of the word, survivors. They knew much about life and how to live it. Their conversation, their attitudes, their conduct—their very lives—were marked by wisdom, humility, dignity, and grace.

The genuine, generous love and the warm welcome these people accorded their young, White, neophyte pastor dispelled any possible disappointment or feeling of superiority I might have had. I took them into my heart as they did me. I had much to learn from them—not just their stories and their history. They became my teachers and life-long friends. My own life was enriched and rewarded during those fifteen years of pastoring in Oklahoma.

I subsequently accepted a dual position in Indiana, requiring the uprooting of my family to serve as college classroom instructor while taking on a leadership role in administration of the LHRAA on VU's campus. I was 39.

After 20 years, I retired from my post as executive officer of LHRAA, still eager to continue my teaching role at the University. Being with the young students was both stimulating and an occasion for my own growing and learning. It was at that time LHRAA's Board voted to move its offices to Milwaukee. To move would mean my withdrawing from the classroom. President Schnabel was inviting me to accept a newly vacated position as the University's Director for Church Relations. I found working in those areas stimulating, providing me and my family with rich experiences among a community of caring colleagues and wonderful neighbors and supportive, thoughtful friends. I wore those two hats from 1981 until my retiring again in 1991. They were busy, demanding, gratifying roles and they were ours to fill.

In 1992–I was 72 then–I accepted the position as first full-time Executive Director of the newly launched Association of Lutheran Older Adults (its acronym title, ALOA, may well sound like a name appropriate for a Hawaiian Travel Agency). This ministry already at its founding defined its purpose as to helping the larger national church bodies and their congregations to recognize and to celebrate the presence of seniors all around us and, where possible, draw on their skills, experiences, and wisdom for enlistment and engagement in useful activity. Its programs were to be prompted and maintained by its brief and challenging theme, CELEBRATE AND SERVE!

Bill Seeber and I had worked together for several years in the university advancement office; I was in Church Relations and Bill in University Development. Good friend, Bill, whose office was near mine, stepped in one morning to visit me. It was a little more than visit. He and a few others were interested in developing a program for older adults. My first response was negative. Didn't see the need for it.

I shared with Bill some of my impressions: some people at 80 are more agile and alert than others at 52; an octogenarian may travel 750 miles to Yosemite, but a 48 year old can't stay awake during a sermon. People think the aging are always talking about their medical/physical needs.

Bill replied: "Some of the very things you've listed haven't even come up in our meetings. Would you be willing to come in and talk to our Board meeting?" I agreed and as we talked the group indicated that they wanted me to direct the Association for Lutheran Older Adults (ALOA).

I served as Executive Director for ALOA until 1997. During this time, I was approached by a friend who suggested a gathering of older adults who loved to sing. Could we have something like an elder hostel and sing beautiful choral music? A musical Lutherhostel?

Our staff worked on this, inviting people we knew who enjoyed choral music to gather in Florida for a four-day song fest. We arranged for Phil Gehring, who for years had been the Valparaiso University chapel organist, to participate. Phil's wife Betty would also come and sing with the group. Retired university choral conductor, Fred Telschow, could direct the choir and both retired professors would also lecture to the group about music on each of the days of the event. There'd be rehearsals each day and evening.

The date was set for November of 1995. The program was developed to include an organ concert by Phil, a choral concert directed by Fred, and a Hymn Sing to be enjoyed by all attendees. The location was Clearwater, Florida–St. Paul Lutheran Church, the home parish of Doris Hanson and Helen Thal.

Invitations were sent out to people who had shown an interest in ALOA and others who might enjoy good music. As the day drew near, the excitement increased. The registrations submitted by the would-be participants were enthusiastic but fewer in number than we had hoped for. More and more, we came to realize that although participants were excited and enthusiastic, the range of voices singing was going to be distressingly unbalanced.

There were a gratifying number of sopranos and a good number of basses, but we would be woefully short of altos and tenors. If this would finally prove to be a high-quality experience, we would need to do some personal recruiting. A telephone call to Elmer Witt in Tacoma, Washington, probed the possibility of enlisting him. Once he agreed, we persuaded the University's Business Manager, Bob Springsteen, another tenor, and his wife Marlise to join us.

Natalie Thiele, whose husband Karl had once been my Associate Director of LHRAA, was living in Florida and she and her sister agreed to participate. Pastor Walter Heyne, now some 92 years old, brother of the Dr. William B. Heyne, founder and conductor of the St. Louis Bach Festival, was excited about what we were offering. We would only be a few hours' drive from where he was now living. And of course there were Dr. Norman and Mrs. Lois Hannewald (he was the former VU Band Director) now living in St. Petersburg. And a few others arrived to save the day. We were breathing more easily.

And then it occurred to me that there might be some former VU students living near Clearwater who might be available and would love music. So I turned to the Valparaiso University alumni directory to see if I might find some other prospects to invite. As I ran my finger down the lists already under the names beginning with "B," I found a familiar one, a Gail whose maiden name had been Jones and now was Blask. Gail, I learned, lived only a matter of minutes from the church where we would be singing. The four days of the event were uncommitted on her calendar and she'd be able to participate.

Meeting with her once more evoked memories of her first days as a student at Valparaiso when she was assigned to the LHRAA office as student aide. As Gail recounts the story:

"I was a former student of Karl's. I was a freshman at VU the same year that Karl and Esther and the boys came. I had worked briefly in the LHRAA office, and then in the Lutze home helping Esther and "baby-sitting" those four boys. When I became engaged to Bill Blask, the first on-campus folks that we told were the Lutzes. Esther loaned me a chain on which to put my engagement ring until after my sorority's "rose ceremony" announcing the engagement.

"I had sadly remembered Esther's sweet friendship when I heard of her struggle with cancer and her death. Esther had battled cancer before in her life. In 1982, cancer attacked this beautiful woman and in the spring of 1994, she became incapacitated by an astral sarcoma, a rare form of cancer. She died in May, 1994, just short of their 49th anniversary. The service, designed by Karl, became a legend at Valparaiso. As good friend Elmer asked, 'Does anyone know the one hymn that was not sung for Esther?' Beautiful readings, music, and finally the Eucharist were shared by the hundreds who attended. The University had lost a beloved mentor, Christian model, and her picture still hangs outside her office in the Chapel of the Resurrection.

"The Lutzes and Blasks had stayed in touch through Christmas letters and such, but after Bill and I divorced, I did not correspond much with anyone.

"It was a wonderful surprise to answer my phone at work and hear a familiar voice. 'This is Karl Lutze.' He told me about the upcoming Lutherhostel. Very convenient since I lived in Largo—just a few miles from the site. And although I taught night school, in addition to working in Child Protective Services for the State of Florida, I would have the time off from work as it was Veterans Day and then the weekend.

"I was excited about the event. I had not seen Karl is over ten years. Good friend, favorite professor!

"The first evening of the Lutherhostel, I had a class to teach, and then hurried over to the church. Entering the choral room, I saw a very red-faced Karl smiling at me. Red faced?—more like burnt. I thought he had foolishly stayed in the sun too long. But soon I learned it was a pre-cancer treatment called Efudex that had caused the redness. But he still looked wonderful. It was a meaningful few days. We sang—had meals together, talked, and I realized that I had real feelings for my former prof. And I thought he did also for me.

"After Karl returned to Valparaiso, he called and we visited on the phone for hours. In January, 1996, there was to be another Lutherhostel in Florida—would I be interested in attending? There was no way I would miss it!

"We spent as much time together as we could at the gathering and by the time he left, we both knew that we wanted to see each other again. In March, I made a trip to Valparaiso. In April, we decided to get married—and during the ensuing months we kept the telephone lines busy.

"A date was finally set for September 27, 1996. Location—Tacoma, Washington. Elmer would marry us there—for free—what a bargain!

"Karl and Elmer did all the arranging.

"We planned for just family, but a few friends were there—Norma and Dennis Gomes from Colorado, and of course, Elmer and Phyllis from Tacoma. And Elmer's children, Barb, Paul, and Frieda were also there.

"All our sons were there: Karl's Peter, Kathe, and their boys, Isaac and Solomon; Steve and Nancy, and their teenagers, Melissa and Nick; Tom and Abby and five-month old Ariana and Mark and Hilda. My son Chris and his wife Donna and baby Damien came from Canada and son Brad and his friend Peter came from Key West. My sisters and their husbands, Sally and Bill and Bess and Joe, brought my mother Minnie to be with us. A few grandchildren were missing; Peter Jonathan and Andrew —Tom's sons and Mark and Hilda's children—Katrina, Elena and baby Matt.

"It was a beautiful wedding at the Church of the Narrows in Tacoma. The next day, we were all treated to a festive brunch at Phyllis and Elmer's with other friends, Luther and Lois Bekemier, and Pauline and Norm Folkers came along to celebrate with us.

"That afternoon, the groom and his sons left us and went to a football game! Their beloved Green Bay Packers were playing the Seattle Seahawks. I had learned that there is nothing that keeps the Lutzes away from the Packers.

"On Sunday, everyone began to depart and we headed off for a wedding trip along the Washington and Oregon coastlines. By early October, we were back home after a wonderful Amtrak train ride across the states to Chicago. We were met in Chicago by friends Bob and Marlise Springsteen and shared a memorable meal at a lovely restaurant before finally arriving back in Valparaiso.

"It's eighteen years later now. I've now lived in Valparaiso longer than I have ever lived in one place.

We've had graduations and weddings and our children have added more grandchildren for us and that makes for much joy.

"Karl retired from ALOA, but stayed active for quite a while helping the young organization. He continues to write and since 1997, he has written four more books (to add to the two completed in earlier years). As the books developed, we both were in publishing and promotion activities. We had wonderful travels all over the US, and even to Europe as Karl did readings from his books and gained a wide following of readers.

"Having 'retired' from children's protective services when we married, I have enjoyed a very different life as pastor's wife, professor's wife, and author's wife. There are plays and concerts to attend and I've done volunteer work with a few organizations.

"The woods, birds and animals provide us with an idyllic setting and I could never want for a more loving, funny, sensitive husband. It's a wonderful partnership. We enjoy University life–especially Chapel and Crusader basketball. And we know that we have been blessed by gracious God. More than eighteen years later, we still love being together!"

On May 8, 2013 Concordia University – St. Paul conferred a Doctor of Letters degree on Karl. It was a wonderful celebration and recognition of Karl's writings and service to our Lord. The four Lutze sons, wives, some grandchildren, and numerous other relatives and friends were on hand in St. Paul for the ceremony and subse-

quent celebration. We both enjoyed the contacts with many friends, family and allies about this event—a chance to review the journey! —Gail

* * * * *

In 1997, I once more retired—this time at age 77. In case you've not been counting the number of times I've retired—it's three. So that at least marks me as having had some experience with retiring. Been there—done that—and I have not yet come to a halt.

We do well to remind ourselves: none of us arrives at senior status without first having spent a good deal of time getting there.

We may not usually think of our earlier years in this way, but in reality, they are the days in which we prepare for our life-work. Learning how to walk, to talk, to communicate—to learn from the experiences and observations of others as we watch, listen, read—to make discoveries in our own experiences—all these are a part of our preparing ourselves for our life-work, the ultimate task of sustaining our lives.

The process begins in the nursery and continues in family life, in social contacts, in formal education situations. Whether that anticipated life-work will be farming, family and home management, dentistry, merchandizing, or any of a wide range of occupations, we find some ways of drawing on what we have learned and what we presume will prove especially gratifying.

We may have discerned latent skills and or special capabilities that seem uniquely ours. This awakening will begin early on as older people ask: "... and what do you want to be when you grow up?" And the child responds, "...drive a fire truck," or "... a baseball player;" or "... a flight attendant;" or "... an astronaut."Of course, as the youngster grows and matures, that career choice may be altered, refined, or replaced a dozen or more times as circumstances and occasions dictate, gradually–or abruptly. The clarified focus launches us into concentrated study–either through formal education or on-the-job training. Then, in most cases, with diploma in hand, we are likely to feel ready to take on our "life-work."

Even then a combination of factors—location, health, new opportunities, family, economic conditions, marriage, parenthood, and a variety of others may prompt people to move in a direction or channel different from what they had earlier envisioned.

* * * * *

Increasingly, as the years pass, and as occasions and opportunities arise, we find ourselves assessing our "life-work" Some measuring points may be:

- Do I feel that I am learning more and growing?

- Is what I'm doing enriching or contributing toward improving the lives of others?

- Do I feel good about what I've been doing this work-day?

- Am I feeling adequately recognized/rewarded for my performance?

Certain occupations are simply not rewarding—neither for finance, fulfillment, nor fun! I can understand why people want to escape jobs that prove monotonous, tedious, or just plain boring—that call for working long hours in unpleasant surroundings. It's not hard to see why such folks want to cry out, "get me out of here," for whom retirement becomes a fleeing from ugliness—who can hardly wait for a life of fishing, golfing, traveling, or opening the doors to all the things their work-life had been denying them.

Feelings of unfinished-ness or that your life has made no real contribution and that you passed through it without being noticed or appreciated can surely derail one's plans for a satisfying future.

By observation—and through my own experience—I have come to realize that people who, once retired, remain productive, whether pursuing a chosen career or finding a new or different avenue in which to perform in a productive way, accept retirement days with far less resentment – and sometimes even with an almost triumphant feeling of successful defiance of the on-slaughts of aging. And, of course, many such choose to postpone retirement because their present work and life style have proved so satisfying.

Long before my retiring, friends of mine who were writers and whose writing I much admired, had repeatedly commented favorably on pieces of mine they had read and urged me, "Don't stop writing, Karl!"

So, retiring sounded inviting to me. I now would have time to write. And that was gratifying. Six books now in all. I felt I was producing.

In my case, I could dismiss the comments of surprise and admiration that others expressed when they became aware of my age. I'd try to chalk off birthdays and anniversaries as not really qualifying as instances of achievement; I would say, "Anyone can have them without any effort, if you stay around long enough!"

Of course, as the years slipped by, I had become aware that I was aging:

- No birthday passes unnoticed in our family;

- My dentist kept adding root canals and crowns;

- Graying of my hair—and less of it;

- Quadruple by-pass surgery;

- Prostate surgery, too;

- Becoming a widower, and

- Taking on new marriage with Gail

And so, you see, my brush with aging through the years might better be termed immersion.

To be sure, I was no longer leaping up stairways, two at a time, or shooting baskets with my grandkids. Arthritis stiffness had kicked in. I developed wrist pain and needed carpal tunnel surgery. And my doctor prescribed medications to hold the symptoms of my Parkinson's disease at bay. That was reality.

However, I could accept all that reality, preferring not to name it "aging," but rather "maturing," "ripening," or "repositioning" or whatever. In one sense, I had not really retired. I hadn't "thrown in the towel." I had now found a "life-work" in my writing.

Increasingly, however, the limitations aging brings with it may become more pronounced. The trembling in my left hand has contributed to a diminishing of my skills at the computer keyboard, necessitating my frequent return to lines I've written, in order to remove redundant letters that have popped up on my screen. The realization that my days are shortening tends to lessen my yen for productivity. I recognize the time I have left to me may not be enough to complete another book. And this in turn alerts me to my need for reflection and a renewed (possibly revised!) definition of "productivity."

Many times, I have stood at the bedside of people who were dying. When I would leave the hospital, I would often muse that I myself might well be closer to death than the person I'd been with–I on my way home might be struck by a truck and my own life be ended.

From all I've read in the Scriptures—and all that I've read in the biographies of famous people and in the newspaper obituaries of local town folk, I cannot predict a precise measurement of anyone's life-span. What is repeatedly clear to me, however, is that the end of life is predictable, certain, and inevitable.

Marking score on achievements in our life-work is ultimately ephemeral—like mist disappearing at the rising of the sun. When the plumber has unplugged so many thousands of clogged drains, the surgeon has successfully performed so many heart transplants, the operatic contralto has sung so many concerts—and they find that their life-work, for any of a variety of reasons, is reduced to retirement dinners, plaques of recognition, or scrap-books of newspaper clippings. When they have lost—or are made to surrender—control of their lives, can we ourselves recognize, and help others recognize an ulti-mate role in our lives; to see that after one's life-work ends, our needs and theirs afford us opportunity for discovering, recognizing and committing ourselves to share in a new life-work—that doesn't require retirement.

It's the work of helping one another in the passing of our time—that gives purpose to all our days.

Addendum:
Inventory of Work Experiences—
The Color of My Parachute

My friend Elmer had been a parish pastor only briefly before he accepted the position of heading up his church body's international youth organization. Support of that ministry dwindled and the Walther League was forced to shut down. There were any number of Lutheran congregations that would readily have called him to be their pastor if they'd known he was available. Some friends suggested he explore possibilities of studying a wide range of options that he might consider. One such surfaced in his participating in a program called *What Color Is Your Parachute?* developed by Richard H. Bolles.

He found the concept very helpful as he considered for himself the question "Where do I go from here?"

By this time, I had through the years received—and declined—thirteen invitations to serve in either a local parish or in some sort of mission structure—both in the states and overseas. Because Elmer had found the Bolles program helpful, he recommended it to me.

The program at one step asked the participant to draw up a list of activities from childhood to the present that demonstrated different skills developed and exercised through the years. I saved my list and I share it here, because it might reveal a part of who I am and what I've been doing these 90-plus years.

The following listing is not intended merely to provide an inventory of achievements. Rather, it is to serve as a reminder of activities that demonstrate experiences drawn upon and developed as previous career(s).

It seems to me that people who may read this, years after I have left the scene, might find this kind of inventory useful as they anticipate their own waning days.

And if some, still young—maybe even a generation or so from now—should stumble across these pages, they might find this kind of inventory helpful for readying themselves for a rich and gratifying vision of the future.

* * * * *

Elementary school:

- 4th grade, president of Sheridan School Harmonica Band

- 8th grade, editor of school paper, *Sheridan Log,* Sheboygan, Wisconsin

Prep school: Concordia Milwaukee

- Advertising manager: *Concordia Courier*

- Blue and White Cheerleader

- *Blue and White Annual* editor

- Member WTMJ Radio Singers

- Door-to-door advertisement distributor

- Pharmacy clerk and delivery
- Dorm director juvenile detention center
- Farmhand, truck driver, threshing team
- Crew member Garton Toy Company and night watchman

Concordia Seminary-St. Louis

- Manager, frozen custard stand
- Floor and door check—roller skating rink
- Railway mails—sorting
- Floor person—department store
- Canvassing for Sunday School program
- Business manager, Male Chorus
- Editing/Advertising Concert Hall
- Brine cooker in pea cannery
- Member *International Lutheran Hour* weekly chorus broadcast

Internship: Baltimore Lutheran City Missions

- Organizing and conducting choir
- Sick-prison, mental hospital visits
- Substitute semonizing in Baltimore churches
- Worship Service accompanist
- Arrangement and conducting of choral music

Parish activities in Oklahoma
Muskogee:

- YMCA African-American branch organizer
- Boy's basketball coach
- Real estate producer and orchestrator of building project
- Involvement in inter-racial concerns
- Developing and conducting direct mail program
- Producing articles for newspapers
- Driving school bus
- Developing creative education materials
- Arranging choral music
- Conducting choir

Pastoral activities
Tulsa, Oklahoma:

- Community survey
- Serving with black community organizations
- Member of founding group as first president of Tulsa Urban League
- Fund raising for new church building
- Cultivating relationships with community leaders
- Preacher and CEO of congregation

Valparaiso, Indiana:
- College-level instructor (Valparaiso University)
- Developing curriculum for human relations studies
- Developing exchange program between VU and Miles College-Birmingham
- Redefined and led University's Office of Church Relations
- Member Board of Directors of National Ministry (LDA)
- Board member Porter County Family Service
- Board member Prisoners and Community Together
- Preparation of Audio/Visual promotion piece
- Counseling of University students
- Helping develop and lead house church
- Authored and published six books
- Consultant to Project Equality
- Managing investments and banking details
- Lutheran Human Relations Association of America
- Editor of *Encore Times* and *The VANGUARD*
- Direct mail funding/promotion
- Planning and administering Annual Institutes
- Workshop planning and director
- Conducting and recruiting for neighborhood workshops

- Organizing and orchestrating fifty nationwide chapters of LHRAA
- Developing and delivering essays at major conventions
- Preparing, submitting proposals for program support
- Fundraising: Breakfast, dinners; one-on-one
- Crisis response
- Contact with church leaders (national and regional)

Providing leadership for developing ministry with Native Americans

- Founding of NILB (National Indian Lutheran Board)
- Participation in councils on demonstrations
- Consultant in racial tension situations

Post-Career

- Became first fulltime Director Association of Lutheran Older Adults (ALOA)
- Produced program materials for congregational ministry with aging adults
- Retired to continue writing, this book being Number Seven.

All to the glory of God.

Biographic Profile
of Karl E. Lutze

After an internship in Maryland in institutional chaplaincy, Karl Lutze was graduated from Concordia Seminary, St. Louis, in January 1945. The following month he was ordained and served the next fifteen years in the South as parish pastor in African American communities, first in Muskogee, Oklahoma, and, subsequently, in Tulsa, where he served as pastor of the Lutheran Church of the Prince of Peace from 1952 to 1959.

In the next 21 years, he served on the staff of the Lutheran Human Relations Association of America, fifteen of those as the Association's executive director. In that same time span he also taught as a member of Valparaiso University's theology faculty. During those years he also planned, coordinated, and taught an exchange program involving students from Valparaiso University as well as students from Miles College (an African American institution of the Christian Methodist Episcopal Church) in Birmingham, Alabama. Lutze was an active member of the Theology Department from 1959 to 1991.

For ten years (1981 to 1991), he served in a full-time capacity with the University as Director for Church Relations while continuing his role at the University teaching theology. During this time he designed an endowed scholarship program at the University and also was consultant to the installation of similar programs for Lakeland College in Wisconsin, for Pacific Lutheran University in Tacoma and two for Concordia Seminary in St. Louis.

Shortly after his retirement from Valparaiso University, he became the first executive director of the Association of Lutheran Older Adults, chartered in 1992. ALOA is an inter-Lutheran ministry involving primarily persons nearing or past 50 years of age, acknowledging added years as gracious gifts.

He was a charter member and twice president of the Tulsa Urban League. He also was a charter member and first president of LuChIP (Lutheran Church and Indian People) and for twelve years a member of the National Indian Lutheran Board and its executive committee. In addition he served two three-year terms as a member of the Lutheran Church—Missouri Synod's Standing Committee on Human Care.

In his service with the Lutheran Human Relations Association of America, he helped organize 50 chapters of this ministry in cities across the country. In that connection, he also conducted four-day workshops for congregations serving changing neighborhoods in seven areas of the country.

In his own community, Lutze helped found and for more than twenty-five years has been a board member of Project Neighbors. This program serves to collaborate with and welcome minority families wishing to make their home in Valparaiso. He has completed almost a dozen years as board member of P.A.C.T. (Prisoners and Community Together) and also has served on Valparaiso University's President's Advisory Committee on Minority Concerns. He has been a board member of the Lutheran Deaconess Association and continues to serve that ministry in an advisory capacity.

He has been named Associate Professor Emeritus of Theology by Valparaiso University and is now Executive Director Emeritus of the Association of Lutheran Older Adults as well.

In addition to being named Honorary Alumnus in 1980, he has been recognized further by Valparaiso University, as co-recipient with the late Professor Walt Reiner, of the Martin Luther King, Jr. Award (1996) as well as co-recipient with his late wife, Esther, of the University's Lumen Christi Medal, its highest award for service. He was the first recipient of ALOA's Celebrate and Serve Award and also received the Seeds of Hope award from Wheat Ridge Ministries. In 2009, Karl Lutze was elected by alumni as one of the 150 Most Influential People in VU history, as the University was celebrating its 150th anniversary.

In 2012, he was awarded the Andrew Schulze Award at Valparaiso University, recognizing his life's work in race relations. On May 8, 2012, he was awarded a Doctor of Letters Degree at Concordia University–St. Paul, MN.

He and his wife Gail reside in Valparaiso, Indiana, where he continues to write, maintaining ties with Valparaiso University and the community.

Index

Abbreviations KEL, LHRAA, MLK, and Valpo stand for Karl E. Lutze, Lutheran Human Relations Association of America, Martin Luther King, and Valparaiso University, respectively. Page numbers for photographs are shown in italics.

Y

Z